Understanding
the
Bible

A Layman's Guide
to the
Historical-Critical
Method

EDWARD J. HAHNENBERG

WingSpan Press

Understanding the Bible: A Layman's Guide to the
Historical-Critical Method

Copyright © 2008 by Edward J. Hahnenberg

Printed in the United States of America
Published by WingSpan Press, Livermore, CA
www.wingspanpress.com
The WingSpan name, logo and colophon are the trademarks of WingSpan Publishing.

ISBN 978-1-59594-267-8

First Edition 2008

Library of Congress Control Number: 2008921013

To the Memory of

POPE PIUS XII

A saintly Pope and brilliant promoter of Biblical research whose encyclicals on understanding the Scriptures have found no equal...

AND

Raymond E. Brown, S.S.

The most learned American biblical scholar in the U.S. A member of the Sulpician Order to which I owe my education in philosophy and religious training...

AND

Augustin Cardinal Bea, S.J.

The most influential Cardinal of Vatican II and whose Mass I had the privilege of attending in Baltimore's Mary Our Queen Cathedral during the Council. His insistence on the faithful having full access to Sacred Scripture complemented his roles as President of the Secretariat for Promoting Christian Unity and as a member of the Pontifical Biblical Commission.

Contents

Introduction

Many sincere Christians read the Bible with the conviction that the world's most popular book is God's Word revealed to mankind for the eternal salvation of the human race. Those of the Jewish tradition consider the Torah (the first five books of the Bible), along with other pre-Christian writings, as divinely inspired by Yahweh. Even the Koran, the sacred book of Islam, admits of divine intervention by Allah in the history of mankind, using names and stories, found in the Bible, familiar to Jews and Christians alike, as an historical basis for the early covenant with mankind by Allah.

Yet in our modern world, there are those who find the Bible a work filled with historical improbabilities. Others question the works included in the Bible as an incomplete list, referring to writings that were left out of the canon, or list, of both the Old and New Testaments.

Recent sensational stories about Jesus, taken from the *Gospel of Thomas*, or the hypothesis that Jesus was married and sired several children, suggested in Brown's *DaVinci Code* and the *Gospel of Mary Magdalene*...even discoveries that purport to be ossuaries with the bones of Jesus and his family...all of these "discoveries" have made the New Testament story of the Christ's bodily resurrection from the dead and ascension into heaven appear to be an incredible tale that cannot stand up to archeological discoveries and scientific analysis.

Confronted with these non-traditional views about biblical works, many Christians retreat into a sort of shell, comforted by their faith in the inerrancy of the Bible, and dismiss any questioning of the Bible's accuracy as the poison of the age in which we live. Christian fundamentalism is on the rise and many Christians prefer to view the Bible as what they have been taught to believe about it...the Bible is God's Word, and that's that.

In the pages that follow, an attempt will be made to examine the Bible using the historical-critical method. Since there is an overwhelming amount of historical-critical analysis still being done today, only the barest of problematic issues are encompassed in this work. Let us begin by defining the term "historical-critical method," its history, and its proponents.

1

The Historical-Critical Method

Definitions draw limits around concepts. No definition is able to be all-inclusive in its few words, no matter how skillfully composed. However, without definitions, there would be indeterminate communication, and misunderstandings would be the rule.

To define the historical-critical method as it applies to understanding the Bible, one might say it is the analytical method biblical scholars use to shed light on the historical processes which resulted in biblical works. The method studies the biblical texts much the same as scholars who study ancient texts from pagan cultures. Without denying the divine revelation attributed to the Bible, scholars using the historical-critical method seek to go back in time and become familiar with the way in which biblical texts were written.

Obviously, God did not use high definition television with Dolby sound to reveal his word to mankind, but rather, by today's standards of communication, a crude, often imperfect, system of revelation which relied on human beings in various times and places to translate that revelation to the written record of their times.

So, when confronted with the story of the origin of the rainbow after the Great Flood, the historical-critical scholar would logically ask "Were there not color refractions in nature before 'the Flood'?" In other words, rainbows are a part of nature, caused by the splitting of white sunlight into its component colors by raindrops. Some of the light that falls on a water drop enters the drop. As it enters the drop, the light is bent (refracted) and split into a rainbow of colors. Rainbows surely existed before the Flood and did not have their beginning with the covenantal story.

One might conclude that the author of Genesis added this detail to highlight the covenantal relationship between mankind and Yahweh, as well as to remind the listener and reader that Yahweh was also a God of hope and not just one of destruction.

Again, when one is confronted with the similarities of the birth of Moses, for example, with that of the Babylonian King Sargon hundreds of years before, the scholar using the historical-critical method asks the question, "Did the human author, or authors, of Exodus draw upon a well-known story from pagan sources to fabricate an historical event which his readers would recognize?" Was there anything known about Moses' birth, or did the author of Exodus have a purpose in describing an event which no one can forget...a cleverly written story of the rescue of an infant who was about to be killed by a ruler, fearful of losing control? The story of the birth of Moses, is similar, interestingly, to the story of King Herod who wanted to kill the infant Jesus. Skeptics might even push the question further... "Did Moses exist at all, or was the author of Exodus a writer of religious fiction?"

Those scholars who use the historical-critical method in understanding the Bible most often operate on the assumption that Moses did exist and that his life had a most important influence on the traditions of the Jewish people.

Going back further, the story of Abraham and his persistence with God in bargaining with Him about whether it was just of Yahweh to destroy Sodom if fifty innocent souls were found there (NAB Gen. 18)...the story is annoying, in a sense to listen to or to read. God agrees with Abraham that He would not destroy the evil city if fifty innocents were found there. Abraham presses God, Who apparently takes the form of a fellow traveler...well, what about forty-five...forty...thirty... twenty...ten. A very patient Yahweh promises not destroy the city if only ten good people are found in "sin city."

The historical-critical scholar might ask: "Was there ever such a discussion, historically, or was this a technique used by the author to show the compassion of God?" To carry the story further, we learn about Lot's wife who looked back as God finally carries out His threat of destruction. She was turned into a pillar of salt. The historical-critical scholar might note that there is a region of salt formations in the area of ancient Sodom which is now buried under the Dead Sea. The evidence of these natural formations might suggest that this story's conclusion is an etiology. Etiologies serve to explain geographic sites.

Off the shore of Leelanau county in northwest Michigan are two islands. These islands are close to a huge sand dune. According to the legend, an enormous forest fire on the western shore of Lake Michigan (now Wisconsin) drove a mother bear and her two cubs into the lake for shelter, determined to reach the opposite shore. After many miles of swimming, the two cubs lagged behind. When the mother bear reached the shore, she waited on the top of a high bluff. The cubs, exhausted, drowned in the lake, but the mother bear stayed and waited in hopes that her cubs would finally appear. Impressed by the mother bear's determination and faith, the Great Spirit created two islands (North and South Manitou Islands) to commemorate the cubs, and the winds buried the sleeping bear under the sands of the dune where she waits to this day.

Many such etiologies derive from ancient cultures. They are legends that are colorful, are memorable for retelling, and serve to explain what ancient cultures did not understand. In the case of the destruction of Sodom, the historical-critical scholar might conclude that the biblical writer had a moral to teach about obedience to God's command, and so might conclude that the story never happened historically, but was passed down to explain the salt formations of pillar-like shapes with a serious lesson at its core.

2

The History of the Historical-Critical Method

In the context of the Christian era, early Church writers such as Jerome and Augustine employed the method. For example, St. Jerome argued with St. Augustine about his translation of the end of the Book of Jonah, having to do with the famous "gourd plant" which grew up to protect Jonah from the hot sun. Augustine accused Jerome of driving one of his congregations out of church because of Jerome's use of "ivy" instead of "gourd." To which comment Jerome let Augustine know that *he* was the scriptural expert and not Augustine. Augustine apparently learned from this and became a biblical scholar in his own right. This famous argument reflected Jerome's concern for accurate translation of the Hebrew into the Latin using textual criticism, a form of the historical-critical method. It is both Augustine and Jerome, as well as later scholars, that Pope Pius XII held up as models for modern exegetes in his encyclical *Divino Afflante Spiritu* (1943).

> *The Fathers of the Church in their time, especially Augustine, warmly recommended to the Catholic scholar, who undertook the investigation and explanation of the Sacred Scriptures, the study of*

the ancient languages and recourse to the original texts.(14)

Wherefore let him diligently apply himself so as to acquire daily a greater facility in biblical as well as in other oriental languages and to support his interpretation by the aids which all branches of philology supply. This indeed St. Jerome strove earnestly to achieve, as far as the science of his time permitted; to this also aspired with untiring zeal and no small fruit not a few of the great exegetes of the sixteenth and seventeenth centuries, although the knowledge of languages then was much less than at the present day. (16)

Divino Afflante Spiritu has rightly been hailed as the "Magna Carta" of modern biblical exegesis, since the pope understood that there were many apparent exaggerations and anomalies in Scripture, especially in the wording of the sacred texts.

For the ancient peoples of the East, in order to express their ideas, did not always employ those forms or kinds of speech which we use today; but rather those used by the men of their times and countries. What those exactly were the commentator cannot determine as it were in advance, but only after a careful examination of the ancient literature of the East. The investigation, carried out, on this point, during the past forty or fifty years with greater care and diligence than ever before, has more clearly shown what forms of expression were used in those far off times, whether in poetic description or in the formulation of laws and rules of life or in recording the facts and events of history. The same inquiry has also shown the special preeminence of the people of Israel among all the other ancient nations of the East in their mode of compiling history, both by reason of its antiquity and by reasons of the faithful record of the events; qualities which may well be attributed to the gift of divine inspiration and to the peculiar religious purpose of biblical history. (36)

Nevertheless no one, who has a correct idea of biblical inspiration, will be surprised to find, even in the Sacred Writers, as in other ancient authors, certain fixed ways of expounding and narrating, certain definite idioms, especially of a kind peculiar to the Semitic tongues, so-called approximations, and certain hyperbolical modes of expression, nay, at times, even paradoxical, which even help to impress the ideas more deeply on the mind. (37)

However, Protestant, Catholic, and Jewish authorities were not always so amenable to questioning the literalness of the scriptures. Galileo, when faced with the scientific evidence he gained through his telescope that Venus had phases, like the moon, and rightly concluded that the earth was not the center of the solar system…this man of faith and science succumbed to the inquisitorial attitude of the Church which upheld, from Scripture, that the sun revolved around the earth, and denounced his own logical conclusions.

The question of whether the Torah contained accurate history was raised by observations that Moses could not have written the Torah by himself, since he apparently records his own death in Deuteronomy (Deut. 34). Readers of the Torah noted other contradictions. It would record events one way, then state that things happened in another order. It would say there were two of something, then, later, fourteen of the same thing. It described Moses going to a Tabernacle before he built it. At first, these problems were explained away by suggestions that, although Moses wrote the Torah, a few lines were added here and there.

A number of scholars during the Middle Ages brought up questions about various lines and passages in the biblical text that seemed odd or out of place:

- Isaac ibn Yashush: An 11th century Jewish court physician in Muslim Spain. He observed that Genesis 36 appeared to be a list of Edomite kings who would have lived long after Moses was dead. He asked why this list was in Genesis.
- Abraham ibn Ezra: A 12th century Spanish Rabbi noted several passages that he thought Moses could not have been responsible for.
- Bonfils: A 14th century scholar located in Damascus. He affirmed ibn Ezra's conclusions.
- Tostatus: A 15th century bishop of Avila. He stated that the passage about Moses' death and others could not have been penned by Moses.

As is turned out, the Catholic Church was not sympathetic to these views. It happened that in the sixteenth century, Catholic Andreas van Maes and two Jesuits, Benedict Pereira and Jacques Bonfrere, suggested that later writers expanded on the writings of Moses. Van Maes' book was placed on Rome's Index of Prohibited Books. British philosopher Thomas Hobbes, during the following century, noted similar problems with Mosaic authorship. French Calvinist Isaac de la Peyrere boldly stated that Moses was not the author of the Torah. His book was banned. Catholic priest Richard Simon, a former Protestant, wrote that the Torah was, at its core, Mosaic, but there were additions and elaborations by scribes. He pointed out the use of doublets (a story being told twice), inconsistencies in content, and differences in style of writing. His book also wound up on the Index.

Notable investigators in the eighteenth century, such as the German minister H.B. Witter, French doctor of medicine, Jean Astruc, German educator J. G. Eichhorn, and graduate student

W.M.L. DeWette, contributed to the theory that the Torah (or Pentateuch) had been written by four writers, or groups of authors, whose work was sometimes found on the same page. According to this hypothesis, four documents had been woven together: that of the Yahwist (J), that of the Elohist (E), that of the Deuteronomist (D), and that of the priestly author (P). Similarly, in the New Testament gospels, a two source theory evolved. There were the synoptic gospels (seen with the "same eye") Matthew, Mark, and Luke which resembled each other, with Mark considered the primary source for Matthew and Luke. Then it was hypothesized that there was a collection of sayings of Jesus called "Q" from the Germen *quelle*, or "source." The Protestant Hermann Gunkel, who died in 1932, maintained that the Torah was a compilation of several writers, but also pointed out that in the Psalms there were different genres of writing, whether legends or hymns. Preceding him was Julius Wellhausen (1844–1918), who held that the Torah had its origins in a redaction of four originally independent texts dating from several centuries *after* the time of Moses.

The Jewish world, too, largely remained aloof. While a few Jewish contemporaries of Wellhausen favored his approach, others wrote polemics against him, trying to undermine his reconstruction of the text's history. These scholars continued to advocate the rabbinic mode of reading, suggesting that what Wellhausen and his colleagues saw as textual contradictions were really not contradictions at all.

These scholars and their theories invited heated discussion. At first they were criticized and maligned. However, their ideas persisted, leading to the acceptance in Jewish, Orthodox, Protestant, and Catholic scholarly circles of the hypothesis that the Torah was not the work of one man, Moses, or by any one person.

As scholars began to study the entire Bible, armed with a better understanding of biblical languages, every book of Scripture was examined both as to authorship and content. One of my teachers of Greek was scripture scholar John P. Weisengoff who demonstrated knowledge of twenty-seven languages. Further, it was scholars such as Raymond Brown, whose *The New Jerome Biblical Commentary* remains a standard reference work utilizing the historical-critical method. Another work utilizing the historical-critical method is *The Anchor Bible Series*, edited by David Noel Freedman. It is a project of international and interfaith contributors, with books by Protestant, Catholic, and Jewish scholars from many countries.

In the Catholic tradition, beginning with the revolutionary encyclical *Divino Afflante Spiritu* by Pope Pius XII in 1943, and followed by Pius' *Humani Generis* in 1950, there culminated in the ecumenical council Vatican II, the document *Dei Verbum*, promulgated in 1965. It stated:

> *To search out the intention of the sacred writers, attention should be given, among other things, to "literary forms." For truth is set forth and expressed differently in texts which are variously historical, prophetic, poetic, or of other forms of discourse. The interpreter must investigate what meaning the sacred writer intended to express and actually expressed in particular circumstances by using contemporary literary forms in accordance with the situation of his own time and culture. For the correct understanding of what the sacred author wanted to assert, due attention must be paid to the customary and characteristic styles of feeling, speaking and narrating which prevailed at the time of the sacred writer, and to the patterns men normally employed at that period in their everyday dealings with one another. (12)*

Thus, the floodgates of biblical research were opened, and no longer was the Bible considered by scholars a collection of writings to be inerrant in matters of history. The Bible is an historical work to be sure, but, most importantly, a collection of works that will continue to merit serious research as to what is moral teaching, history, parable, poetry, or whatever genre of writing used by its many authors.

3

Faith and the Historical-Critical Method

Today, many who read the Bible in light of sensational "discoveries" or theories that debunk the resurrection of Jesus from the dead or that suggest that Jesus married and had children, usually take one of two positions: One, that the New Testament relates one of the biggest frauds perpetrated upon mankind...or two, that these notions are the work of clever entrepreneurs who have their eye on the money that a book or a movie will generate in a secular society, and that all of this rewriting of Christian tradition is just so much fluff with no historical substance to it.

In the case of the first group, there are no arguments that can convince that Jesus is, and always was, divine. There are no physical proofs of a resurrection and the miracles reported in the Gospels, in their view, either never happened or are naturally-explained phenomena. As for stories in the Old Testament, the first group equate most of them with mythological tales of other ancient religions. This group may grant the existence of rulers such as David in ancient Israel, but as for Moses, for example, there is no corroborating evidence from sources other than the Torah that there was such a man, or if there was, "the truth is greatly exaggerated."

In the case of the second group, the Jewish, Christian, and

Muslim traditions have been around for millennia, and there are commonalities that abound. In the view of the second group, Adam and Eve were real people…Abraham was real…Moses worked miracles…etc. The Torah, New Testament, and Koran are sacred books revered by over a half of the world's six billion plus population. Obviously, these Abrahamic religions have their differences in beliefs, but many events recorded in the Torah and New Testament are accepted in the Koran, for example. Christians accept the Torah, but only minimal portions of the Koran. Jewish adherents are mostly at odds with the Koran and New Testament. However, the three religions are monotheistic, with Abraham a binding personality in all three.

While these two groups have their supporters, there are many who are just unsure about this story or that in the Bible. Most people find the Bible inspiring on a moral level or as an important collection of literature which has moved mankind to the foundation of Western legal mores. Others hold to a sort of relativism about the Bible which equates the sacred writings of all world religions as having worth for mankind for various sociological reasons.

But what about the Bible as the word of an uncreated being called Yahweh, God, Jesus, or Allah? Is this compilation of many kinds of literature really divinely inspired, and, if so, how is it inspired?

In the Torah, Yahweh appears as an all-knowing being who interacts with mankind with both kindness and fierce anger. He promises a covenant of loyalty with mankind, but singles out one group of people, the Hebrews, for his special attention. He speaks through prophets, warning the Hebrews of the danger idolatry, then punishes them and sends them into exile. He even wipes out the entire human race, save for Noah and his family, prior to his covenant with the Hebrews.

What kind of God is this Yahweh? As we saw above, he

waffles when confronted by Abraham. He gives Moses the Ten Commandments, but then chooses to act through wars and even asks Abraham to murder his son Isaac.

Is it not strange that the God of the Torah is quite different from God's Son, Jesus Christ…so much so that Marcion, quite possibly a Christian bishop, in the second century AD taught that the god of the Old Testament, Yahweh, was not the true God but rather that the true and higher God had been revealed only with Jesus Christ. Marcion was one of the first to promulgate a *canon*, or list, of divinely inspired books. He wanted nothing to do with the Old Testament as regards divine inspiration.

Today, most believing Christians hold that Jesus Christ is truly God and that God, in the fullness of being, is a Trinity of divine persons: Father, Son (Jesus), and Holy Spirit. Where in the gospels are these beliefs clearly stated? Nowhere. It took the early church several centuries before this basic doctrine was settled upon. There are those today who *read back into the gospels* the doctrine of the Trinity, using the text from Matthew (c. 28) or the divinity of Christ (John c. 1), and others, to prove their point. It was not so clear back then, however. What is certain about the early centuries of Christianity is that the early church writers, for the most part, held to the tradition that God is a coeternal Trinity, and, despite the extremely influential Arian heresy which held that Jesus was created by the Father and not coeternal with him, codified this belief in the councils of Nicea (325) and Constantinople I (381). (Muslims have always rejected the divinity of Christ.)

The latest official statement from the Roman Catholic church regarding the historical-critical method is to be found in the Pontifical Biblical Commission's *The Interpretation of the Bible in the Church* (1993). In the document's Preface, Joseph Cardinal Ratzinger, now Pope Benedict XVI, observed:

> *In the history of interpretation, the rise of the*

historical-critical method opened a new era. With it, new possibilities for understanding the biblical word in its originality opened up. Just as with all human endeavor, though, so also this method contained hidden dangers along with its positive possibilities: The search for the original can lead to putting the word back into the past completely so that it is no longer taken in its actuality. It can result that only the human dimension of the word appears as real, while the genuine author, God, is removed from the reach of a method which was established for understanding human reality.

The document itself calls the historical-critical method "the indispensable method for the scientific study of the meaning of ancient texts." It further notes that: "Holy Scripture, inasmuch as it is the 'word of God in human language,' has been composed by human authors in all its various parts and in all the sources that lie behind them. Because of this, its proper understanding not only admits the use of this method but actually requires it." (I, A)

So, in the largest branch of Christianity, Catholicism, the historical-critical method has found a home. Not that it was always so. Papal encyclicals and statements prior to Pius XII, such as Leo XIII's encyclical on biblical study and Pius X's decree *Lamentabili* (1907), seemed to cling to a much narrower view regarding the historical-critical method. *Providentissimus Deus* (1893) by Leo XIII, for example, warned:

It follows that those who maintain that an error is possible in any genuine passage of the sacred writings, either pervert the Catholic notion of inspiration, or make God the author of such error. And so emphatically were all the Fathers and Doctors agreed that the divine writings, as left by the hagiographers, are free from all error, that they labored earnestly, with no less skill than reverence, to reconcile with each other those numerous passages which seem at variance—the very passages which in great measure have been taken up by the "higher criticism;" for they were unanimous in laying it down, that those writings, in their entirety and in all their parts were equally from the afflatus (divine inspiration) of Almighty God, and that God, speaking by the sacred writers, could not set down anything but what was true. (21)

While Leo cautioned scholars to accept the divine inspiration of Scripture, he opened the door a crack by admitting the need of a knowledge of science in helping explain the difficulties in interpreting scripture. Leo correctly pointed out that ancient writings from history were accepted as true without much scrutiny, whereas biblical writings were automatically doomed to error if a disagreement was found with non-biblical records. If one remembers that during the nineteenth century Darwinism had pitted science against established religion, it is not surprising that church authorities felt threatened when it came to making an about face and agreeing with science's attack on religion itself.

Since Vatican II in the 1960s, we have seen new translations of the Bible with Protestant, Catholic, Orthodox, and Jewish scholars working side by side. Mainline Protestant scholars have pretty much accepted the historical-critical method. However, fundamentalists in the evangelical denominations have not. "Classic" fundamentalism was built around a set of "fundamentals" of the faith that, it was assumed, all Christians would believe. However, the single idea of the absolute inerrancy of Scripture emerged as the defining feature of fundamentalism following the 1920s.

In his first book as pope, *Jesus of Nazareth (2007)*, Pope Benedict, while once again praising the historical-critical method, calls for a union of faith and scientific inquiry as regards the Word. The Holy Father acknowledges that the historical-critical method is indispensable for serious analysis, and recognizes it has unearthed a large body of materials and knowledge that enable us to reconstruct the figure of Jesus with a depth that, only a few decades ago, would have been unthinkable. But it is only through faith, he maintains, that one can come to understand that Jesus is God. Interestingly, the pope, a renowned theologian in his own right states about his book in the Forward that: *It goes without saying that this book is in no way an exercise of the magisterium, but is solely an expression of my personal search "for the face of the Lord."*

The use of the historical-critical method in regards to the Old Testament, however, brings up many controversial problems. In the next few chapters, we will look at Old Testament personalities and stories with the eyes of one who has faith it as God's divine revelation to mankind, but also of one who finds many of its stories hard to believe.

4

Genesis
Chapters 1–11

...The first eleven chapters of Genesis, although properly speaking not conforming to the historical method used by the best Greek and Latin writers or by competent authors of our time, do nevertheless pertain to history in a true sense, which however must be further studied and determined by exegetes; the same chapters,...in simple and metaphorical language adapted to the mentality of a people but little cultured, both state the principal truths which are fundamental for our salvation, and also give a popular description of the origin of the human race and the chosen people. If, however, the ancient sacred writers have taken anything from popular narrations (and this may be conceded), it must never be forgotten that they did so with the help of divine inspiration, through which they were rendered immune from any error in selecting and evaluating those documents. (HG, 38)

The above excerpt from Pius XII's *Humani Generis*, was an important statement for biblical exegetes in the decades since 1950. Pius tried very hard to provide a connection with Leo XIII and Pius X as regards their views regarding interpretation of scripture, while at the same time providing scholars the freedom to investigate whether the sacred author(s) of the stories in Genesis 1–11 drew upon pagan sources for the sacred text.

In those chapters, after all, we are confronted with the primal stories of the creation of the world, Adam and Eve, the Garden of Paradise, Original Sin, Cain and Abel, the Nephilim, Noah and the Flood, the tower of Babel, and a preliminary history of Abraham. The historical-critical scholar may ask whether these stories are based upon a type of symbolic rhetoric...*a metaphorical language adapted to the mentality of a people but little cultured.* Pius is all but saying that the "popular narrations" are pagan stories, from which the Mosaic author(s) drew information.

So, did Adam and Eve exist? What about Original Sin? Did Noah endure a real Flood? Was there a Tower of Babel? Is the beginning of the Torah pagan in its origins based upon a dimly remembered past that the Hebrew author(s) adapted to their religious beliefs? These are indeed tough questions for the person of faith who may have been brought up in an educational environment that accepted the biblical accounts as true history.

5

Adam and Eve

Until the advent of the understanding of DNA, evolutionists scoffed at the idea that the human race descended from one set of biological parents. The idea that there could have been many Adams and many Eves is called *polygenism*.

Enter Eve. In 1987, Allan Wilson, Rebecca Cann, and Mark Stoneking, researchers at the University of California-Berkeley, catapulted mitochondrial DNA into the headlines worldwide when they announced that they had traced it back 200,000 years to the oldest female ancestor of living humans—an African woman quickly dubbed Eve. Eve's debut rocked the archaeological community, which had been arguing for decades over whether modern humans evolved on more than one continent or instead swept out of Africa to replace more archaic hominids around the world. Wilson's group was attacked for sloppy science, and in fact there were problems with the original calculations. But genetic data from dozens of researchers have since almost universally supported the "Out of Africa" theory. "History has made a pretty consistent stamp on populations," says Lynn Jorde, a geneticist at the University of Utah, who has found African roots in nuclear DNA as well as in mitochondria and the Y. "Looking at more and more of the nuclear DNA is going to clarify the picture."

There is much work to be done in the study of genetics, and there may never be conclusive scientific evidence that *monogenism* (one Adam and Eve), as related in Genesis, really happened.

However, many in the scientific community have given some credence to the African Eve; however, the question of Adam is still up in the air. Some in the scientific community contend that Adam lived tens of thousands of years later, because of the *y-chromosome* issue. Y-chromosomal Adam probably lived between 60,000 and 90,000 years ago, judging from molecular clock and genetic marker studies. While their descendants certainly became close intimates, Y-chromosomal Adam and mitochondrial Eve are separated by at least 30,000 years.

Finally, is there any evidence to stand in the way of an hypothesis that would posit the following scenario: Mitochondrial Eve did not have a human soul, with any self-awareness but mated with a male hominid. This continued down through time until such time as God infused self-aware human souls into descendants of mitochondrial Eve and Y-chromosomal Adam. These two would have lived in a state of innocence with above-average intelligence as the biblical narrative suggests...until the fall.

Enter faith. While science gives us some tantalizing evidence that humans descended from an African Eve (white supremacists, take note), Pius XII pointed out in *Humani Generis* that:

> *When, however, there is question of another conjectural opinion, namely polygenism, the children of the Church by no means enjoy such liberty. For the faithful cannot embrace that opinion which maintains that either after Adam there existed on this earth true men who did not take their origin through natural generation from him as from the first parent of all, or that Adam represents a certain number of first parents. Now it is no way apparent how such an opinion can be reconciled with that which the sources of revealed truth and the documents of the Teaching Authority of the Church propose with regard to original sin, which proceeds*

> *from a sin actually committed by an individual Adam and which, through generation, is passed on to all and is in everyone as his own. (37)*

It must be pointed out that papal encyclicals, in and of themselves, are not considered infallible by any authority in the Catholic Church, including popes or church councils. However, this statement by Pius is one that Catholics cannot dismiss as inconsequential, since it references a dogma held by the Church as infallible, namely the existence of Original Sin, and thus the ordinary necessity of Baptism to remove it. Protestants, Orthodox Christians, Jews, and Muslims have their own opinions about papal writings and the existence of a monogenistic Adam and Eve.

6

The Great Flood

A skeptical approach might be to discount the biblical account of the Great Flood as folklore or as a fairy tale. The historical-critical scholar would probably point to the *Epic of Gilgamesh* as a pagan story from which the writer of Genesis would have drawn most his material. *The Epic of Gilgamesh* is one of the oldest written stories known. It comes to us from ancient Sumeria, and was originally written on twelve clay tablets in cuneiform. It is about the adventures of the historical King of Uruk (somewhere between 2750 and 2500 BC). Tablet XI (the Flood Story) has come down to us intact, containing some three hundred lines. The original date of composition is placed in the *Ancient Near East Texts* at the turn of the second millennium BC, if not earlier.

In both the Genesis and Gilgamesh stories:

- The Genesis story describes how mankind had become obnoxious to God; they were hopelessly sinful and wicked. In the Babylonian story, they were too numerous and noisy.
- The gods (or God) decided to send a worldwide flood. This would drown men, women, children, babies and infants, as well as eliminate all of the land animals and birds.
- The gods (or God) knew of one righteous man, Ut-Napishtim or Noah.
- The gods (or God) ordered the hero to build a multi-story wooden ark.

- The hero initially complained about the assignment to build the boat.
- The ark would be sealed with pitch.
- The ark would have with many internal compartments.
- It would have a single door.
- It would have at least one window.
- The ark was built and loaded with the hero, a few other humans, and samples from all species of other land animals.
- A great rain covered the land with water.
- The mountains were initially covered with water.
- The ark landed on a mountain in the Middle East.
- The hero sent out birds at regular intervals to find if any dry land was in the vicinity.
- The first two birds returned to the ark. The third bird apparently found dry land because it did not return.
- The hero and his family left the ark, ritually killed an animal, offered it as a sacrifice.
- God (or gods) smelled the roasted meat of the sacrifice.
- The hero was blessed.
- The Babylonian gods seemed genuinely sorry for the genocide that they had created. The God of Noah appears to have regretted his actions as well, because he promised never to do it again.

There are many differences between the two stories also. However, the commonalities are striking. It is generally accepted the Gilgamesh story was written before the story of Noah.

The Great Flood was a very unusual and singular event in its telling. Because of the magnitude of destruction, it would have left an indelible and permanent mark on the minds of any survivors. This story would have been told and retold, passing down from generation to generation. Over 600 of these stories throughout the entire world have been carried down to the present age.

So, was the Great Flood a world-wide event or an account of a local or regional flood, of which there were many in world history. Silt deposits several feet deep, caused by flooding, have been found in numerous places in Mesopotamia. However, both the Gilgamesh and Genesis stories indicate a world-wide event.

An interesting theory has been put forth by James A. Marusek as published in the Cambridge-Conference Network (CCNet), Issue 47/2003 of 29 May 2003). According to Marusek, analysis of staghorn coral (a coral that always grows in shallow water) provides evidence that the ocean level rose 400 feet since the end of the last Ice Age and the Ice Age came to an abrupt end approximately 11,650 years ago. This occurred when global temperatures rose approximately seven degrees C. Marusek explains that during the last Ice Age, large areas of the continents were covered in glacier ice sheets. Strong jet streams moving north/south made it difficult to grow crops and scratch out a living in many locales and environments. However, shallow coastal lands were among the richest and most fertile on Earth. These protected coastlines were the sites of the largest cities and population centers. This is not much different than today, where 85 percent of the Earth's population and the majority of cities are within 200 miles of the coastline.

Enter an asteroid or major tectonic plate shift. If a comet or asteroid landed in an ocean, and, since there are several sites that are possible candidates, there is more reason to suspect it hit in a large body of water, the tsunami effect would have inundated coastal regions dramatically. This event would not have left evidence such as the Yucatan Peninsula strike which occurred some 65,000,000 years ago. That event is credited with initiating a global conflagration which, according to some scientists, would have killed the dinosaurs in about twenty minutes.

There are other theories about the Great Flood. Some investigators have claimed that there was a great boat which was swallowed up by a glacier and is still on Mt. Ararat in Turkey. However, the flooding necessary in order to raise a craft to mountainous heights is impossible to explain. Rain alone simply could not raise global levels to such a height. In any case, the Great Flood story appears to have had as its basis a real event dimly remembered and passed on down through many cultures. So, if the flood was a global event, a tsunami flooding coastal regions would have more credibility and would explain why there are flood stories from every continent.

Regarding North America, before the Vikings or Columbus set foot here, native peoples had been living in America. When the Europeans came here, there were probably about 10 million natives populating America north of present-day Mexico. And they had been living in America for quite some time. It is believed that the first native Americans arrived during the last ice-age, approximately 20,000–30,000 years ago through a land-bridge across the Bering Sound, from northeastern Siberia into Alaska . The oldest documented Indian cultures in North America are Sandia (15000 BC), Clovis (12000 BC) and Folsom (8000 BC).

Here is a sampling of flood legends from around the world, taken from the Northwest Creation Network website (http:// www.nwcreation.net/noahlegends.html):

AFRICA

Southwest Tanzania
Once upon a time the rivers began to flood. The god told two people to get into a ship. He told them to take lots of seed and to take lots of animals. The water of the flood eventually covered the mountains. Finally the flood stopped. Then one of the men, wanting to know if the water had dried up let a dove loose. The dove returned. Later he let loose a hawk which did not return.

Then the men left the boat and took the animals and the seeds with them.

ASIA

China

The Chinese classic called the Hihking tells about "the family of Fuhi," that was saved from a great flood. This ancient story tells that the entire land was flooded; the mountains and everything, however one family survived in a boat. The Chinese consider this man the father of their civilization. This record indicates that Fuhi, his wife, three sons, and three daughters were the only people that escaped the great flood. It is claimed that he and his family were the only people alive on earth, and repopulated the world.

Babylon

Gilgamesh met an old man named Utnapishtim, who told him the following story. The gods came to Utnapishtim to warn him about a terrible flood that was coming. They instructed Utnapishtim to destroy his house and build a large ship. The ship was to be 10 dozen cubits high, wide, and long. Utnapishtim was to cover the ship with pitch. He was supposed to take male and female animals of all kinds, his wife and family, provisions, etc. into the ship. Once the ship was completed the rain began falling intensely. The rain fell for six days and nights. Finally things calmed and the ship settled on the top of Mount Nisir. After the ship had rested for seven days Utnapishtim let loose a dove. Since the land had not dried the dove returned. Next he sent a swallow which also returned. Later he let loose a raven which never returned since the ground had dried. Utnapishtim then left the ship.

Chaldean

There was a man by the name of Xisuthrus. The god Chronos warned Xisuthrus of a coming flood and told him to build a boat. The boat was to be 5 stadia by 2 stadia. In this boat Xisuthrus was to put his family, friends and two of each animal (male and female). The flood came. When the waters started to recede he let some birds loose. They came back and he noticed they had mud on their feet. He tried again with the same results. When he tried the third time the birds did not return. Assuming the water had dried up the people got out of the boat and offered sacrifices to the gods.

India

A long time ago lived a man named Manu. Manu, while washing himself, saved a small fish from the jaws of a large fish. The fish told Manu, "If you care for me until I am full grown I will save you from terrible things to come". Manu asked what kind of terrible things. The fish told Manu that a great flood would soon come and destroy everything on the earth. The fish told Manu to put him in a clay jar for protection. The fish grew and each time he outgrew the clay jar Manu gave him a larger one. Finally the fish became a ghasha, one of the largest fish in the world. The fish instructed Manu to build a large ship since the flood was going to happen very soon. As the rains started Manu tied a rope from the ship to the ghasha. The fish guided the ship as the waters rose. The whole earth was covered by water. When the waters began subsiding the ghasha led Manu's ship to a mountaintop.

AUSTRALIA

There is a legend of a flood called the Dreamtime flood. Riding on this flood was the woramba, or the Ark Gumana. In this ark was Noah, Aborigines, and various animals. This ark eventually came to rest in the plain of Djilinbadu where it can still be found. They claim that the white man's story about the ark landing in the middle east is a lie that was started to keep the aborigines in subservience. This legend is undoubtedly the product of aboriginal legends merging with those of visiting missionaries, and there does not appear to be any native flood stories from Australia.

EUROPE

Greece

A long time ago, perhaps before the golden age was over, humans became proud. This bothered Zeus as they kept getting worse. Finally Zeus decided that he would destroy all humans. Before he did this Prometheus, the creator of humans, warned his human son Deucalion and his wife Pyrrha. Prometheus then placed this couple in a large wooden chest. The rains started and lasted nine days and nights until the whole world was flooded. The only things that were not flooded were the peaks of Mount Parnassus and Mount Olympus. Mount Olympus is the home of the gods. The wooden chest came to rest on Mount Parnassus. Deucalion and his wife Pyrrha got out and saw that everything was flooded. They lived on provisions from the chest until the waters subsided. At Zeus' instruction they re-populated the earth.

NORTH AMERICA

Mexico

The Toltec natives have a legend telling that the original creation lasted for 1716 years, and was destroyed by a flood and only one family survived.

Aztec—A man named Tapi lived a long time ago. Tapi was a very pious man. The creator told Tapi to build a boat that he would live in. He was told that he should take his wife and a pair of every animal that was alive into this boat. Naturally everyone thought he was crazy. Then the rain started and the flood came. The men and animals tried to climb the mountains but the mountains became flooded as well. Finally the rain ended. Tapi decided that the water had dried up when he let a dove loose that did not return.

United States

The Ojibwe natives who have lived in Minnesota since approximately 1400 AD also have a creation and flood story that closely parallels the Biblical account. "There came a time when the harmonious way of life did not continue. Men and women disrespected each other, families quarreled and soon villages began arguing back and forth. This saddened Gitchie Manido [the Creator] greatly, but he waited. Finally, when it seemed there was no hope left, the Creator decided to purify Mother Earth through the use of water. The water came, flooding the Earth, catching all of creation off guard. All but a few of each living thing survived." Then it tells how Waynaboozhoo survived by floating on a log in the water with various animals.

Delaware Indians—In the pristine age, the world lived at peace; but an evil spirit came and caused a great flood. The earth was submerged. A few persons had taken refuge on the back of a turtle, so old that his shell had collected moss. A loon flew over their heads and was entreated to dive beneath the water and bring up land. It found only a bottomless sea. Then the bird flew far away, came back with a small portion of earth in its bill, and guided the tortoise to a place where there was a spot of dry land.

SOUTH AMERICA

Inca

During the period of time called the Pachachama, people became very evil. They got so busy coming up with and performing evil deeds they neglected the gods. Only those in the high Andes remained uncorrupted. Two brothers who lived in the highlands noticed their llamas acting strangely. They asked the llamas why and were told that the stars had told the llamas that a great flood was coming. This flood would destroy all the life on earth. The brothers took their families and flocks into a cave on the high mountains. It started to rain and continued for four months. As the water rose the mountain grew keeping its top above the water. Eventually the rain stopped and the waters receded. The mountain returned to its original height. The shepherds repopulated the earth. The llamas remembered the flood and that is why they prefer to live in the highland areas.

There are many texts and websites which offer similar flood stories. A website which recounts hundreds of these stories is http://www.talkorigins.org/faqs/flood-myths.html (*Flood Stories from Around the World* by Mark Isaak, last revised 2002.)

7

The Tower of Babel

The biblical account makes several points:

- Everyone spoke the same language.
- Mankind was migrating east.
- In order that mankind be remembered, the suggestion to build a city and a tower that reached to the sky was carried out.
- The Lord went down to see the city which was being built.
- The Lord appears threatened by the ambition of mankind's project.
- He decides to confuse their speech, so they could not understand each other.
- The city building stops and the people scatter all over the earth, with different languages.

For the historical-critical scholar, the Tower of Babel is both an etiology and a story based on an actual structure, the *ziggurat*. One of the most important aspects of Babylonian religion and tradition, and probably the best known, is the ziggurat.

Ziggurats were huge "stepped" structures, like square layer cakes, with, on their summit, far above the ground, a temple. This Temple would often have been dedicated to the city god. The ziggurat would easily have been the most conspicuous building in the city, towering above any visitors coming to their city. Therefore the ziggurat was not just a religious center but also a center of civic pride. The ziggurats were built on an immense scale: in the time of Hammurabi they would sometimes reach the height of 150 feet.

Put yourself in Babylon during the Great Exile (587–539 BC). You, as a learned Hebrew, would have been exposed to several religious and moral influences, not the least of which was the Code of Hammurabi, extant in Babylon at least a thousand years before the Exile.

Babylon was the great melting pot for pagan gods and goddesses as well. Babylonian religion was a polytheistic system of belief common throughout Mesopotamia. Of the thousands of recognized gods, only about twenty were important in actual practice. The most important are reviewed here.

Anu, Enlil, and Ea, were patron deities of the oldest Sumerian cities and were each given a share of the Universe as their dominion. Anu, god of the heavens and patron god of Uruk (biblical Erech; Genesis 10:10) did not play a very active role. Enlil of Nippur was god of the earth. The god of Eridu, Ea, was lord of the subterranean waters and the god of craftsmen.

After the political rise of Babylon, Marduk was also considered one of the rulers of the cosmos. The son of Ea and patron god of Babylon, Marduk began to attain the position of prominence in Babylonian religion in the time of Hammurabi. In subsequent periods, Marduk (Merodach in Jeremiah 50:2) was considered the leading god and was given the epithet Bel (equivalent to the Canaanite term Baal), meaning "lord" (Isaiah 46:1; Jeremiah 50:2; Jeremiah 51:44). Marduk's son Nabu (the Nebo in Isaiah 46:1), god of the nearby city of Borsippa, was considered the god of writing and scribes and became especially exalted in the Neo-Babylonian Period.

Astral deities—gods associated with heavenly bodies—included the sun-god Shamash, the moon-god Sin, and Ishtar, goddess of the morning and evening star (the Greek Aphrodite and Roman

Venus). Sin was the patron god of Ur and Haran, both associated with Abraham's origins (Genesis 11:31). Ishtar, the Canaanite Astarte/Ashtaroth (Judges 10:6; 1 Samuel 7:3–4; 1 Kings 11:5), had a major temple in Babylon and was very popular as the "Queen of Heaven" (Jeremiah 7:18; Jeremiah 44:17–19).

The Hebrew scribes who likely composed much of the Old Testament did so during the Great Exile in Babylon. They borrowed from pagan religious writings and etiologies, always, however, with the focus that Yahweh or Elohim alone created and maintained the universe.

The Tower of Babel in Genesis was quite possibly the ziggurat built in Babylon at the time of Hammurabi. However, there is a large amount of documentation of the ziggurat that existed in the time of Nebuchadnezzar II (605–562 BC) who deported the Jews.

This was a ziggurat already old by the time of his reign and could have been the same as the ziggurat that existed in the reign of Hammurai who ruled Babylonia from 1795–1750 BC. Its Babylonian name was "Etemenanki" (see below) which means in English "House of the platform of Heaven and Earth".

We have a Babylonian tablet that gives us the dimensions of the ziggurat at the time of Nebuchadnezzar II. The ziggurat's condition declined and it was in ruins when Alexander arrived in 331 BC.

Thanks to a tablet that has been found we are in the possession of most of the dimensions of the ziggurat:

1st layer: 300ft by 300ft 110ft high
2nd " 260ft by 260ft 60ft high
3rd " 200ft by 200ft 20ft high
4th " 170ft by 170ft 20ft high
5th " 140ft by 140ft 20ft high
6th " No information given
7th layer: 70ft by 80ft 50ft high

The Babylonian scribe omitted the dimensions of the sixth step but its height was probably twenty feet.

The main structure of the ziggurat was trodden clay but there was a layer of bricks on the outside. The top of the ziggurat was reached by a broad stairway going up the side. This stairway was said to be thirty feet wide. Around the base of the ziggurat was a line of buildings. These were storerooms and accommodation for priests and others connected with the temple.

The Jewish writer of Genesis 11 could have explained the beginning of languages by means of the physical structure before his eyes, casting the story with an important but additional teaching that Yahweh disapproved of man's pride and idolatry.

8

The Abrahamic Stories

There is no corroborating evidence from the contemporaneous written record of other cultures that the primal patriarch of Judaism, Abraham, existed. The name, yes; the person, no. Yet the Bible and the Koran accept his existence as historical fact. Although the biblical stories about Abram, or Abraham, often contain didactic moral tales about the man and his descendants, both the Torah and the Koran have different takes on "who was to inherit what" of the Promised Land.

The Islamic holiday, Qurbani Id (or Id Al-Adha), is known as the "Sacrifice Festival." Muslims celebrate this "great feast of sacrifice" on the tenth day of the last month of the Muslim year. According to their doctrinal schema, this day celebrates the willingness of Abraham to sacrifice his son Ishmael born to Abraham's barren wife Sarah's maid Hagar.

If you remember the Old Testament account, you will be somewhat perplexed. Was not Isaac, born miraculously later to Sarah, the one whom God instructed Abraham to offer? The difference is this. Christians accept the testimony of the Bible. Muslims reject the Bible and believe the Koran (or Qur'an) contains the inspired, uncorrupted record.

Although the Koran does not name the child whom Abraham was to sacrifice, Muslims believe it was Ishmael, and they believe that idea is supported by the Koran. So, Muslims believe that Ishmael was to inherit the Promised Land of Israel, not Isaac. Jews, obviously, opt for Isaac. And so the disagreement goes on to this day, with very bloody consequences in the West Bank, Gaza, and, for that matter, in much of the Arab / Jewish world.

According to Jewish belief, Jewish history begins in the first half of the second millennium BC. According to the traditions of the Jewish people, 4,000 years ago, near the Mesopotamian city of Ur, a nomadic sheepherder named Abraham rebelled against the pantheon of local deities and proclaimed his belief in one, omnipotent, indivisible God. In the Hebrew scriptures, the Bible, this God commanded Abraham to "go forth from your father's house to the land that I will show you." God promised Abraham the land of Israel and prosperity to his descendants, in return for following his commands. Having made this covenant, Abraham set out with his extended family, or tribe, and settled in the Promised Land.

Many years later, when famine beset the peoples of Canaan, Abraham's grandson Jacob brought the tribe, now known as Israelites, to Egypt where work and food were plentiful. After an initial period of prosperity, the Israelites were reduced to slavery, and remained in bondage for four hundred years. But, we are getting ahead of ourselves...

According to *The New Jerome Biblical Commentary*, the historicity of the patriarchs...and, thus, their stories...Abraham's included, has been debated.

> *Wellhausen proposed that the (Abrahamic) stories were a retrojection from the period of the monarchy... Dominance of the literary-critical method with its focus on the J and E documents of the monarchical period reinforced scholarly skepticism about the historicity of the stories. Countering the skepticism of the literary critic, archaelogical and epigraphic finds from the ancient Near East in the century since Wellhausen have produced many parallels to the names, customs, and literary genres of the stories.*

The individual parallels are often difficult to assess. Taken together, they do not prove the historicity of the patriarchs but rather make plausible the general setting of the stories. One solid piece of evidence is the proper names. The names Abraham, Ishmael, and Jacob are attested in 2ⁿᵈ millennium texts; they are not given to Israelites in the OT period....It is possible that the ancestors were part of a large Amorite migration that founded dynasties in N Syria and Mesopotamia at the beginning of the 2ⁿᵈ millennium. (JBC 2, 17)

Were Abraham, Isaac and Jacob real persons? Are their stories factual or legendary, embodying a fictionalized history of the Hebrews, symbolizing the way the Hebrews looked back at their nomadic origins from the vantage point of their settled life in Canaan? Archaeological contributions provide no definite clues for determining whether or not these men ever existed. A Babylonian business contract from the beginning of the second millennium B.C. refers to a certain Abarama (Abraham), son of "Awel-Ishtar," but there is no possible way to link him with the Abraham of the Bible. Two Abrams, one associated with Egypt and the other with Cyprus, are mentioned in Ugaritic administrative texts. The references demonstrate that the name was known in the periods often associated with the patriarchs. The name of Jacob appears as the name of a Hyksos king (Ya'qob-er) about 1700 B.C. and, in an Egyptian list from the time of Pharaoh Thutmose III (ca. 1480 B.C.), a Palestinian town called Jacob-el (Ya'qob-el) is found, but these inscriptions do not help us very much.

So, what is one who uses the historical-critical method to believe? How far does faith need to enter in, when there is minimal credible history in such stories of Abraham down to Moses...a period of over half a millennium at the very least? As a minimum, the stories in the Torah show the covenant relationship between God and the Hebrews. For those following the Judeo-Christian tradition, the stories certainly have moral value and have traditionally been considered divinely inspired and free of moral error.

Yet, if Yahweh, the author of life, commanded the sacrifice of Abraham's son, would that not contradict the most basic of moral imperatives that life is sacred? Because the story is so often tied to the Christian belief that it prefigured God the Father's willing that His Son be sacrificed on the cross, Christian writers rarely have questioned the Old Testament story, especially since Yahweh is seen as testing Abraham's faith.

The author of Hebrews makes the point clearly:

> *By faith Abraham, when put to the test, offered up Isaac, and he who had received the promises was ready to offer his only son, of whom it was said, "Through Isaac descendants shall bear your name." He reasoned that God was able to raise even from the dead, and he received Isaac back as a symbol.* (New American Bible:, Heb. 11:17–19)

Yet, how much of such intertestamental explanation is inerrant? When one looks at the genealogies of Jesus in the Gospels of Matthew and Luke, no credible scholar would accept them as having serious historical value. They are constructs, both with different lists of several fictional ancestors, which the evangelists used to tie Jesus to David. Certainly, not inerrant as regards history…The historical-critical scholar understands all of that, and so looks with a critical eye on intertestmental and intratestamental explanations of related biblical texts.

There are important moral truths for the believer in the explanation given in Hebrews.

- God is the creator and lawgiver.
- If God asks martyrdom of a human being, that is His right.

- God can raise from the dead.
- The story prefigures the death and resurrection of God's Son.

The issue that muddles the story is God (or his messenger) asking Abraham to kill his son. Not nice. However, let it be pointed out that God spared Abraham the gruesome act. Problem solved. Blessings ensue. All is well.

History or fiction? We simply do not know. Is faith required here or the skeptical questions of the scripture scholar? Maybe a little of both? For most, it is not an issue.

9

The Moses Era: An Overview

As was intimated earlier, scripture scholars, in the majority, come down on the side of the conclusion that Moses was a real person. For most of the two millennia of the Christian era, Moses was thought to have authored the Torah or Pentateuch.

Then, as we have seen, questions arose about his authorship, and the condemnations by the Church began, then waffling, and, finally, acceptance of later authors as the real writers of the books. One thing is certain. Someone or some group or some combination thereof did write the Torah. Scholars have identified the J, E, D, and P passages quite nicely, even approximating the centuries these writers or groups of writers composed and edited the first five books of the Bible.

Yet, how much of Moses do we know, really? Certainly we can read of his role and exploits in the Torah. However, is Moses mentioned in any other culture's contemporaneous written record? Is Moses found in the hieroglyphs of Egypt? No, not even one iota is found outside the Torah.

Moses is such a central figure in Jewish, Christian, and Muslim history that it would be hard to imagine that the man is a fictional superhero. The historical-critical scholar, however, if true to the method, must examine not only the historicity of Moses, but the stories associated with him…his birth, his conversations with Yahweh on a mountaintop, his learning of Yahweh's name, his reception from God of the Ten Commandments, the plagues inflicted on the Egyptians, his leading the people through the sea, the sojourn in the Sinai, his laws…everything is the domain of the historical-critical scholar.

Before an examination of the wonders (10 plagues) recounted in Pharaoh's presence and the crossing of the sea as Moses led the people out of Egypt, let us examine how the Israelites got themselves into servitude in Egypt. The Bible explains that Joseph, son of Jacob (aka Israel), grandson of Isaac, and great-grandson of Abraham, was sold by his brothers to a group of Ishmaelites going to Egypt for twenty pieces of silver (Gen. 37). After rising to prominence in the Pharaoh's court, a famine ensued for Jacob's family and they went to Egypt in search of food, since the Nile delta was a dependable source of grain. After an intriguing story of deception involving his brothers, Joseph reveals himself and promises to give his family the best land in Egypt, in the land of Goshen, (which has not been definitely identified even today.) Joseph's father Jacob, and his extended family (not counting women) of sixty-six descendants, migrate to Egypt where they become a "numerous and powerful" people. Egypt's new Pharaoh, who knew nothing of Joseph, sees the Israelites as a threat, so he calls his midwives (Hebrews Shiphrah and Push) to kill the infant boys, but not the girls. (NAB: Ex. 1)

Enter Pharaoh's daughter. The baby, to be called Moses, is saved by the royal daughter and given, unknowingly, to Moses' mother for nursing and upbringing.

Egypt, in the Bible, holds a unique reputation. It is at once a friend, then an enemy. It is Egypt which accepted small groups of Asiatics which found a refuge from famine, such as the extended family of Joseph. Yet, in its history it was the Egyptians who fought immigrants for control of their own land. The historicity of the Exodus narrative is a complex issue. There are at least two major hypotheses which date the Exodus. One is based on excavations in the Nile Delta that have shown that as early as the nineteenth century BC, large numbers of Canaanite immigrants (descendants of Jacob?) began to settle there, building towns similar to those in Canaan (modern day Israel). By the mid-seventeenth century, the Semitic population in northern Egypt had gained political control. From 1650 to 1550 BC, this domination widened south to most of Egypt. These Semites only adopted some Egyptian cultural characteristics. Native Egyptians called Semite kings *heqaw khasut*, translated into Greek later as "Hyskos."

A resurgence of Egyptian power by native rulers in Thebes in Dynasty 17 (1590–1549 BC), eventually led to a revolt against the Hyskos in the north, in which the Egyptians re-established control. Following the beginning of Dynasty 18 (1540–1070 BC), the pharaohs of the New Kingdom of Egypt not only subdued the Hyskos in the south, but moved north into Canaan, as far north as modern day Syria. Using boats to sail up the coast of Canaan, Thutmose III (1479–1425), saved a trek through Canaan and landed on the coast of Syria. From there the Egyptians won major battles in Syria, crossing the Euphrates. However, the victories were tenuous at best and boundaries, upon the death of Thutmose, were established wherein Egypt kept control of the Canaanite coast as far north as Ugarit (in today's Lebanon).

However, control of modern day Israel by Egypt was not to be forever. Harsh attacks by Hittites, from modern day Turkey, during the reign of Rameses II (1279–1213 BC), and, later by groups called "Sea Peoples," which included the Philistines, drove Egypt out of "the Promised Land."

Back to the two major hypotheses:

The first is that the Exodus occurred when the Hyskos were driven out of Egypt during the rise of the New Kingdom. This hypothesis suggests that the original Hebrews were synonymous with the Hyskos, or at least part of them, and that the Exodus occurred in the 1500s BC.

The second is that the Exodus occurred during the reign of Rameses II in the 1200s BC. Intensive archaeological research has shown a gradual growth of small rural settlements in the hill country of southern Canaan from around 1200 BC. If descendants of those in the Exodus began their settlement as the Egyptian control of lands north of the Nile Delta began to unravel, then the biblical wanderings in the Sinai would have occurred in the mid-1200s. In addition, several sites west of the Jordan River were destroyed around this time. Were these actions those of the Hebrews? How much of the growth of rural settlements and destruction of established sites was brought about by the migrations and/or invasions of newcomers to Canaan specifically by Israelites is still, archeologically, an open question.

Conclusion:

It may be concluded that there was an influx into Israel of some sort of group of migrants in the 1500 to 1200s, mostly settling in the hill country, away from the "Sea People" who lived on the eastern coast of southern Canaan.

H. Norman Whybray notes in his book *Introduction to the Pentateuch*, Eerdmans. 1995:

> *Subsequent scholars have differed about the causes of such an internal movement of population but have held on to the general theory (e.g., Gottwald, The Tribes of Yahweh, 36–41; Niels P Lemche, Early Israel, 41 Iff; Giovanni Garbini, History and Ideology in Ancient Israel, 64). But if the present Moses story is largely a purely literary creation, a question arises concerning the origin of the*

religion of Yahweh which the Pentateuch so closely associates with the figure of Moses. Some proponents of the "internal development" hypothesis, though rejecting the notion of a mass immigration, have conceded the possibility that although the origins of the Israelite people as a whole must be looked for on the soil of Palestine, there may have been a small group of people (sometimes known as "the Moses group") who had been slave laborers in Egypt, had made their escape, and had then arrived in Palestine, having both in Egypt and on their journey undergone some experiences associated with a god named Yahweh who had in some way been their deliverer. It was this small group which, having been absorbed into the newly formed people of Israel, had introduced the worship of Yahweh to their new compatriots. Such a theory might account for the fact that some of these traditions seem to have been known, especially to the eighth-century prophet Hosea and his northern audience. But this would not account for a Pentateuchal narrative concerning an army of 600,000 men with their families, augmented by a further "mixed crowd," and accompanied by numerous flocks and herds, who supposedly walked through the desert under the direction of Moses for forty years.

Why should the Pentateuchal author have concocted such a story, and why did it eventually come to be so universally accepted by later Jews as the basis of their beliefs about their origin and their relationship to God? It must be remembered that the Pentateuch as we have it now is on any reckoning a document written many centuries after the time when the events that it describes are purported to have occurred. Consequently, unless there were strong oral traditions about that remote era which strongly contradicted the Pentateuchal story, there is no reason why it should have been disbelieved. There may well have previously been little or no such "folk memory." It must further be remembered that the Pentateuch was probably the first comprehensive account of Israelite origins to be written, at about the same time as such works became fashionable in the civilized world. Some Jewish literature of a later period—midrashes, apocalypses, "testaments," and the like—show that many people were ready to believe much more extravagant stories about Israel's origins and early history than this.

Moreover, as has already been noted with regard to Genesis, such a story—of a generation which was so wonderfully saved and protected by its God, yet because of its sin and rebelliousness was in the end denied access to the land which had so long been promised—would convey both a welcome assurance of God's supreme power over the nations of the world and also a warning message to a postexilic generation which did not yet repossess that land, that only if it was obedient could it expect further benefits from its God. If the Pentateuchal story was new to that generation, it was extremely relevant to its situation. That it has been so completely accepted as a true account by countless generations of the Jewish people is a tribute to its literary merit and compelling power. (Whybray, 68,69)

This point of view is shared by authors of the *Oxford History of the Biblical World.*

Some future historical or archaeological discovery

46

EDWARD J. HAHNENBERG

may provide concrete, indisputable evidence for the historicity of the biblical Exodus. Until then, however, the details of the biblical Exodus narrative...will continue to be debated. Admittedly, we cannot prove that the Exodus took place; but we also cannot prove that it did not. As with so much else in the Bible, belief or disbelief in the historicity of the Exodus narrative becomes a matter of faith. (OHBW, 120)

A note about R. Norman Whybray: Whybray, a noted British priest and eminent historical-critical Old Testament scholar of the Anglican Church, born in 1923, was a key figure in the life of the Society for Old Testament Study for over thirty years. He was President of the Society in 1982, and Editor of its Book List from 1974 to 1980. Though his works, especially in the OT Wisdom literature, are still highly respected in the academic community, he was frequently faulted by the reviewers for the comparative weakness of his alternative proposal, that the Pentateuch was essentially the work of a single author.

47

10

The Parallel
Moses Birth Story

We have referred, twice before, to the incident of Moses' birth. There is the familiar biblical story. Then, there is an uncannily parallel story in the historical record of Agade's King Sargon. The city of Agade, or known otherwise as Akkad, was an ancient city located in modern day Iraq. It was well known for its fertile location right between the Euphrates and Tigris rivers. Unfortunately this intriguing site is still undiscovered. The birth story of Moses, probably recorded during the tenth century BC, and possibly edited by P compiler during the Exile, reflects the pattern found in the birth account of King Sargon of Agade who lived near the end of the third millennium B.C. The Sargon account reads:

> Sargon, the mighty king of Agade, am I.
> My mother was a changeling, my father I knew not.
> The brothers of my father loved the hills.
> My city is Azupiranu, which is situated on
> the banks of the Euphrates.
> My changeling mother conceived me, in secret
> she bore me,
> She set me in a basket of rushes, with bitumen
> she sealed my lid.
> She cast me into the river which rose not over me.
> The river bore me up and carried me to Akki,

the drawer of water.
Akki, the drawer of water, lifted me out
as he dipped his ewer.
Akki, the drawer of water, took me as his
son and reared me.
Akki, the drawer of water, appointed me as
his gardener.
While I was a gardener, Ishtar granted me
her love,
And for four and...years I exercised kingship. (Ancient Near East Texts, 119)

The similarity of the Moses and Sargon accounts is obvious. Actually both stories reflect literary patterns often associated with heroes. The life of the hero is threatened when he is still a child; he escapes; he is unrecognized until he achieves his full status as a leader of the people. Very often his life pattern reflects the way in which a people consider their early history, for they look back upon their humble and difficult beginnings and marvel at what they have become. The life of the hero embodies the struggle of a nation or a group to achieve greatness. Having detected the hero motif in the Moses literature, one must consider the question of how much of the Moses cycle may be labeled "legend," and how much "history." To further complicate the discussion, there is an opinion that Sargon and Moses are both drawing on a common archetype and that both stories are fictional....kind of like an undiscovered "Q" source.

11

The
Ten Commandments

Since the historical-critical scholar has only the book of Exodus for the story of Moses' life, what was known of him came down largely through oral tradition, culminating in a final redaction around the time of the Exile. "The Ten Commandments," the 1956 movie directed by Cecile B. DeMille and starring Charlton Heston as Moses, has left a visual impression that is both memorable and yet quite fundamentalist in its following of the events described in Exodus. Aaron, according to Exodus, was Moses' mouthpiece since Moses had a speech difficulty. Moses, however, said to the LORD, "If you please, LORD, I have never been eloquent, neither in the past, nor recently, nor now that you have spoken to your servant; but I am slow of speech and tongue." (NAB: Ex. C. 4: 10)

The 50s movie gives little time to Aaron, but rather focuses on a powerful Moses. This impression of Moses...tall, commanding, eloquent, and charismatic...is likely the impression that our generation has of the man, and, quite possibly, the view of the storytellers who passed down the traditions about him.

Whatever the case, Moses is a larger than life figure in Jewish history, for it was he that conversed with Yahweh, received from God the Ten Commandments, and brought the Israelites to the Promised Land.

The Ten Commandments are foundational to Western legal

systems, and are a legacy most scholars attribute to Moses' encounter with Yahweh. Yet there are some scholars who maintain that a prior code, that of Hammurabi, was the source for the Ten Commandments. The Hammurabi code, written around 1750 BC by the famous Babylonian king, would have been well known to the final redactors of the books of Exodus and Deuteronomy during the Exile. Naturally, the historical-critical investigator is faced with the question: Did the authors of the Torah borrow from this local code and create the story of Moses on Mount Sinai?

There are 282 laws in Hammurabi's Code. Below are listed laws 1–15:

1. *If any one ensnare another, putting a ban upon him, but he can not prove it, then he that ensnared him shall be put to death.*

2. *If any one bring an accusation against a man, and the accused go to the river and leap into the river, if he sink in the river his accuser shall take possession of his house. But if the river prove that the accused is not guilty, and he escape unhurt, then he who had brought the accusation shall be put to death, while he who leaped into the river shall take possession of the house that had belonged to his accuser.*

3. *If any one bring an accusation of any crime before the elders, and does not prove what he has charged, he shall, if it be a capital offense charged, be put to death.*

4. *If he satisfy the elders to impose a fine of grain or money, he shall receive the fine that the action produces.*

5. *If a judge try a case, reach a decision, and present his judgment in writing; if later error shall appear in his decision, and it be through his own fault, then he shall pay twelve times the fine set by him in the case, and he shall be publicly removed from the judge's bench, and never again shall he sit there to render judgment.*

6. *If any one steal the property of a temple or of the court, he shall be put to death, and also the one who receives the stolen thing from him shall be put to death.*

7. *If any one buy from the son or the slave of another man, without witnesses or a contract, silver or gold, a male or female slave, an ox or a sheep, an ass or anything, or if he take it in charge, he is considered a thief and shall be put to death.*

8. *If any one steal cattle or sheep, or an ass, or a pig or a goat, if it belong to a god or to the court, the thief shall pay thirty fold therefore; if they belonged to a freed man of the king he shall pay tenfold; if the thief has nothing with which to pay he shall be put to death.*

9. *If any one lose an article, and find it in the possession of another: if the person in whose possession the thing is found say "A merchant sold it to me, I paid for it before witnesses," and if the owner of the thing say, "I will bring witnesses who know my property," then shall the purchaser bring the merchant who sold it to him, and the witnesses before whom he bought it, and the owner shall bring witnesses who can identify his property. The judge shall examine their testimony—both of the witnesses before whom the price was paid, and of the witnesses who identify the lost article on oath. The merchant is then proved to be a thief and shall be put to death. The owner of the lost article receives his property, and he who bought it receives the money he paid from the estate of the merchant.*

10. *If the purchaser does not bring the merchant and the witnesses before whom he bought the article, but its owner bring witnesses who identify it, then the buyer is the thief and shall be put to death, and the owner receives the lost article.*

11. *If the owner do not bring witnesses to identify the lost*

article, he is an evil-doer, he has traduced, and shall be put to death.

12. If the witnesses be not at hand, then shall the judge set a limit, at the expiration of six months. If his witnesses have not appeared within the six months, he is an evil-doer, and shall bear the fine of the pending case.

[There is no 13th Law because, then as now, the number 13 was considered to be unlucky.]

14. If any one steal the minor son of another, he shall be put to death.

15. If any one take a male or female slave of the court, or a male or female slave of a freed man, outside the city gates, he shall be put to death. (ANET: 166)

In 1901, three fragments of black diorite were found 200 miles east of Babylon. After being fitted together, they formed an impressive round-top stele or pillar, which stands about 7.5 feet high. This came to be known as the Law Code of King Hammurabi, considered one of the most significant legal documents from antiquity. The stele is now kept at the Louvre in Paris, France.

A relief on the upper face of the stele depicts the king in worship before the sun-god on a throne. The code begins with a prologue, followed by a listing of the laws. The discovery of the stele was particularly important to Bible scholars. Some historical-critical scholars reasoned that the Mosaic law in the Bible was derived from the Code of Hammurabi. Most scholars, however, have abandoned this theory, since further research has shown that, in ancient times, there were codes of law in various countries. Some of these were even older than Hammurabi's stele.

Furthermore, Mosaic law moved beyond the Code of Hammurabi, or any of the ancient law codes, because it is grounded in the worship of one God. The ethical principles in the law of Moses spring from love toward the one true God.

Such love demands that one also love fellow human beings, whom God made in his image. Moses thus talks about human sin and our responsibility to God in resisting sin. Hammurabi and other ancient law-givers, however, do not address this issue.

As for the laws in Leviticus, to say they are of divine origin might be rejected by some historical-critical scholars. For example, the "kosher" laws of "clean and unclean" foods had nothing to do with undercooked pork and trichinosis. Pork meat was cooked and eaten without ill effects by non-Israelites.

Most likely, the clean and unclean foods revolved around those birds and animals which were scavengers, or which were thought not to have been fit for the Garden of Eden. Then, too, pork might have been rejected as a sign to the pagans that the Hebrews were a chosen people...indeed, circumcision played a similar role of identification.

So, did Moses receive the Ten Commandments from God in a face-to-face encounter? Faith affirms it and nothing in historical-critical research has surfaced to counter the biblical story. It is, however, interesting to note that in the fourteenth century BC, Egypt's official religion was monotheistic, due in large part to the Pharaoh Akhenaten (1364–1347 BC). According to this Pharaoh, the god Ra created himself from a primeval mound in the shape of a pyramid and then created all other gods. Thus, Ra was not only the sun god, he was also the universe, having created himself from himself. The effect of these doctrines can be seen in the sun worship of this Pharaoh, who became an uncompromising monotheist.

12

The Plagues

Exodus (c. 9–11) records ten plagues: Water to blood, frogs, gnats, flies, death of livestock, boils, thunder and hail, locusts, darkness, and death of the firstborn. Again, the book of Exodus paints these events as miracles, direct interventions by Yahweh to convince Pharaoh (no specific Pharaoh is mentioned) to free the Israelites from a life of slavery, highlighted by their work as builders using clay bricks.

Speaking of bricks, Pharaoh punishes the Israelites by withdrawing the use of straw in order to make the work harder... presumably the bricks would break more easily. However, straw was not used in many clay brick buildings in the ancient world, as is the case today. The punishment may have been an author's addition to dramatize the story.

The Hebrew words for what is commonly understood as *miracle* by many today did not have the same meaning then as today. The English word miracle comes from the Latin *miraculum* "something to be wondered at." The Hebrew words that are translated into English as *miracle* are *mopet* (symbolic sign) and *ot* (sign), neither of which need refer to anything marvelous.

> *...the Bible does not view nature as a closed system of laws. The ordinary workings of nature are often attributed directly to God: storm, famine, and plague...(even today, natural catastrophes are called "acts of God"). There is little sensitivity to secondary causality, and the distinction between the*

natural and the supernatural is frequently tenuous.
The biblical notion of the miraculous includes acts
that are explicable on the level of human interaction
as well as those that are not...If there are Old
Testament stories of stupendous incidents...the
principal OT miracle is the deliverance of Israel
from Egypt, in itself an action governed by historical
forces. But the biblical authors look upon such a
historical event with the eyes of faith and in it the
miraculous action of God...(JBC 81: 93)

So, what are we to make of the 10 plagues...It is the fundamentalist view that the events occurred exactly as described. Yet, God is a master of timing, and, while direct intervention by God in the lives of mankind appears limited on the surface even today, personal testimonies of peoples of faith are strong throughout the ages that God performs miracles every day. In Catholic belief, Lourdes in France is the site where miracles of heart, mind, soul, and body occur often...witness the six million people that visit there each year. Yet, officially, the Catholic Church, since the 1858 apparitions of Mary to Bernadette Soubirous, has given approval to less than seventy healings as true, unexplained miracles.

The conclusion, therefore, of the historical-critical scholar, as regards the 10 plagues of Egypt, might logically be that events such as described in Exodus did happen, but not in the modern-day understanding of *miracle. It is to be noted that Abraham, by his lie to a Pharaoh in Egypt about his wife being his, caused plagues also to occur.* (NAB: Gen. 12: 17)

It may be, as some scholars hold, that the plagues were unusual, but that there are natural explanations of them. For example, commentators are divided as to whether the water was really changed into blood, or whether only a phenomenon was produced similar to the red discoloration of the Nile during its annual rise, which gave the water the appearance of blood. The latter view is now commonly accepted.

Several of the following plagues could be contributing factors for the plague that followed. For example, the fifth plague, pestilence, could follow the demise of the fourth plague's flies and gnats (3rd plague) which could have arisen following the death of frogs (2nd plague).

The ninth plague was a horrible darkness which for three days covered all Egypt except the land of Gessen. The immediate cause of this plague was probably the hamsin, a south or south-west wind charged with sand and dust, which blows about the spring equinox and at times produces darkness. http://www.catholic.org/encyclopedia/view.php?id=9413.

Countering these arguments for a natural explanation of many of the plagues is the consideration that most of them were produced at Moses' command, and ceased at his prayer, in one case at the time set by Pharaoh himself. Purely natural phenomena, it is clear, do not occur under such conditions. Moreover, the ordinary phenomena, which were well known to the Egyptians, would not have produced such a deep impression on Pharaoh and his court. (COE, ibid.)

Suffice it to say that science can offer only so much by way of explanation of these phenomena, however the Exodus account does have exaggerations. We will examine one, the crossing of the Red (or Reed) Sea in the following chapter.

13

The Crossing

Theoretically, it should be possible to reconstruct the route taken by the Israelites out of Egypt. However, it is as yet virtually impossible.

> *As a structured, literary genre, the itineraries for a distinct genre within the Pentateuch (Torah) belong to a literary form widely attested in the ancient world. The primary function of the genre, which survives mostly in official documents, is to describe routes...ancient itineraries (in nonbiblical examples) customarily provided a complete and reasonably reliable record of the routes described... already in ancient times the locations of many of the places in the Exodus itineraries appear to have been lost. Of the approximately three dozen or more localities mentioned, few can be pinpointed on the ground, and none of the places listed in Egypt or the Sinai Peninsula can be situated with confidence.* (OHBW, 90)

The Red Sea crossing presents, both in Exodus and in modern movies, an image of the miraculous. We know that Ramses II had horses and chariots. In Qantir village, also in Sharkiya, a German-Egyptian archaeological team located the horse stables of Ramses II, covering around two acres of land.

"This is the biggest and oldest horse stable ever found in the world," claims Gaballa Ali Gaballa. Gaballa goes on to explain that the stables were found on the site of the 3300-year-old city of Piramesse (Per Ramses, or "house of Ramses"), 115 kilometres northeast of Cairo. The stables, sub-divided into several rectangular areas, each with its own gate, were built by the king to breed more than 400 horses for purposes of war, hunting and recreation.

This recent discovery is still far from proving the envelopment of Pharaoh's "chariots and charioteers" in water "like a wall to the right and the left."

An example of exaggeration is the Israelites' crossing the Red Sea, where, by the way, no one is certain what place is referred to. Presumably it was at the headwaters of the Red sea, now referred to as the Reed Sea which has since disappeared because of the Suez Canal water diversion. The common misinterpretation of the Hebrew *y'am Suf* is the "Red Sea," so it was thought Moses crossed the Red Sea. If this really happened, they really crossed the Reed Sea, the real meaning of *y'am Suf.*

In the biblical account of the crossing...*The Israelites set out from Rameses for Succoth, about six hundred thousand men on foot, not counting the children.* (NAB, 12:37).

If we take literally the number of Israelites crossing any given point, the number of people might well have exceeded 2,000,000, not to mention animals, belongings, etc. The crossing was made on foot in one night. It is difficult to image such a massive exodus of people across any stretch of dry sea bed in that time frame, what with babies, the elderly, slow moving beasts of burden, and the sheer number of potty stops along the way. The historical-critical scholar might see a bit of exaggerated triumphalism in the account.

As with many of the numbers in the Bible there is symbolism that is obvious. The numbers 3, 7, and 12 can be literal numbers, but more often they represent completeness. The number 7, and its multiples, are used several hundred times in the Bible.

Just what 6, or its multiples, (600 of Pharaoh finest chariots and drivers perish, plus all the rest of his chariots and charioteers in his army…600,000 men on foot cross the sea) means is unclear, but it no doubt had some sort of symbolic significance…perhaps of imperfection, being one less than 7.

What Egyptian records show is that Egypt regularly allowed groups of tribes to pass in and out of Egypt in times of famine. The Exodus crossing was written down several hundred years later and includes elements of J, E, and P composition and redaction, so the final version in Exodus was subject to many hands. (JBC 3, Intr.)

Whybray observes:

> To what extent it was the author of the present Pentateuch who created the "biography" of Moses is not clear. In view of the methods which he employed in Genesis, it is reasonable to accord him a large part in this. From the literary point of view it is clear that it is the figure of Moses which now holds the story together and gives it a focus. Many of the stories are quite short, and it seems probable that these could have already been circulating in the author's time; not all of them need have been originally connected with Moses himself. But if Moses was already revered as lawgiver, it is not surprising that other great events should have been attributed to him, notably the Exodus, the miracle at the Sea, and the journey toward the Promised Land. (Whybray, Introduction to the Pentateuch, 67.)

More on the "invasion" of Canaan by Joshua and his successors later…

The Jerome Biblical notes that there were ten plagues to test the Egyptians, just as there would be ten tests of the Israelites in the desert. (JBC 3: 26)

14

The Golden Calf

Although it is not listed as one of the ten tests in the desert, much is made of the idolatry of the Israelites in Exodus 32. Yahweh's delivery of the Ten Commandments to Moses in the third month after the crossing of the Reed Sea was followed by the promulgation of much of the Mosaic social and religious legal system as well as the construction of the Ark of the Covenant (NAB: Ex. chapters 21–31).

Chapter 32 finds Moses' delaying coming down from Mt. Sinai with the two tablets of stone inscribed by Yahweh himself. The people, in consultation with Aaron, decide to forge a golden calf to represent Yahweh, since no one knew whether Moses would return. On the mountain, God got angry and threatened to destroy the Israelites. Moses appealed to Yahweh with various arguments, and God relented. However, upon Moses' reappearance, he finds the people celebrating, offering holocausts and peace offerings to their newly-fashioned God. Moses breaks the tablets and forces the people to grind up the golden calf, spread the gold dust on water, and drink up. After questioning his brother, Moses orders the slaying of about three thousand of the Israelites.

What is the historical-critical scholar to make of all this? There are many inconsistencies and duplications in the story which scholars have been aware of. However, the problems have not all been resolved. The story obviously casts aspersions not only on the Israelites but on Moses' brother Aaron as well.

On the face of it, the story exposes a dim-witted people and an extremely pusillanimous leader in Aaron...hardly the 40 day change expected of a people who had been miraculously delivered from Egypt and had been provided with a reliable source of food in the on-going appearance of the manna and quail.

Was there another explanation for their actions, or was it the redactors' narrative that was fabricated to teach a lesson?

Consider the world the Israelites had lived in. The worship of bulls was part of Egyptian culture. The cult of the bull started at the very beginning of herds. The bull was a protector of the deceased, and linked to the pharaoh, symbolizing the king's courageous heart, great strength, virility, and fighting spirit. Yahweh had only recently revealed himself to Moses. The creation of an image of the Egyptian bull-god Apis would have been a natural course of action to represent a higher divine power.

Then there is the later use of the term *El, "the bull,"* to designate Yahweh. The Hebrew word used in Exodus is "elohim"...the plural form of *El. Interestingly, we find "elohim" in Genesis.* In the Ugaritic culture, El was the "head god". The religion of Ugarit and the religion of ancient Israel were not the same, but there were some striking similarities. For example, the name of the ultimate divine authority at Ugarit was El, one of the names of the God of Israel (e.g., Gen 33:20). El was described as an aged god with white hair, seated on a throne. However, at Ugarit, El was sovereign, but another god ran things on earth for El as his vizier. That god's name was Baal, a name quite familiar to anyone who has read the Old Testament.

However, two time periods are being discussed here. One, the actual age of the Exodus (somewhere in the 15th–12th centuries BC), and, two, a period in which Exodus was ultimately redacted (the Exile—6th century BC). How could the freed exiles have

EDWARD J. HAHNENBERG

known anything of the Ugaritic culture, which came to use "el" in their mythology perhaps centuries later?

Dr. Michael S. Heiser, Academic Editor, *Logos Bible Software*, notes in his personal commentary:

> It is often said that one of the most important principles of interpretation is to put every text into its proper context. That is, to read the text to be interpreted in place with its surroundings: the surrounding text as well as the social, historical, cultural, and literary traditions of the world in which it was produced. The texts recovered at Ugarit provide a key piece of literary, social, and religious context for certain passages of the Old Testament.
>
> First of all, it's important to understand that the biblical writers, though under the inspiration of the Holy Spirit, followed the ordinary forms of literature that were current in their day when they wrote. If, for example, the biblical writer was describing a covenant treaty between God and his people, his description conforms in style to covenant treaties known elsewhere in the ancient world. To depart from this style would have seemed strange to the ancient readers: "What kind of covenant treaty is this? Didn't this guy know how to write one?" The apostle Paul as well wrote his letters to the churches in a recognizable style and with an expected format. The recipients of Paul's letters knew what a letter was supposed to look like. Just as we wouldn't write a letter home to Mom and put footnotes in it, or jot down a recipe and lace it with legal mumbo-jumbo, so the biblical writers wrote using the literary conventions and forms that would be expected by their audience. Biblical writers didn't just use the forms of contemporary non-inspired literature; they were also influenced by the literature itself. Just as preachers

today quote commentaries, journals, news periodicals, or even television shows to drive home or illustrate a point, so the biblical writers used external material to draw attention and make a statement...The people of biblical times knew the quoted material wasn't inspired, but it had meaning for them and their audience.

So, is it unreasonable to suppose that, if there were Elohist redactors of Exodus, they used the term for Yahweh that they were familiar with? Jesuit Mitchell Dahood, in his three volume translation of the Psalms, makes a strong case for the Ugaritic influence on the Psalms. His translations often substitute *El* for Yahweh. More on Dahood's work, which is quoted in the Jerome Biblical Commentary nearly fifty times, in a later chapter.

The historical-critical observer might view the story of the golden calf as more of an act of celebratory worship of a god that had set them free, and whom they as yet knew very little of, rather than an act of idolatry as painted in Exodus.

The moral lesson of the story, however, is clear. Yahweh establishes his predominance as the one true God, and monotheism is firmly reinforced as the religion of the Jewish people.

15

The
Conquest Hypothesis

The Book of Joshua is filled stories of conquest of the Promised Land, beginning with the famous siege of Jericho. Then the Israelites captured Ai, which led to the formation of a confederation of tribes to ward off the feared onslaught of the conquering Hebrews. Joshua 9 lists the confederacy groups... the Hittites, Amorites, Canaanites, Perizzites, Hivites, and Jebusites.

Joshua 10 paints a gruesome picture of Joshua's army putting to the sword the king and every person in Makedah. The Israelites did the same to the king of Libnah, "leaving no survivors." Chapter 13 lists thirty-one kings and their peoples conquered, from the south to the north of the Promised Land. Presumably every person was killed, in a massive, terrifying onslaught of inhabitants in large and small villages, which were called "kingdoms."

According to the Bible, this abhorrent disregard for human life in the name of Yahweh is how Israel came to be a nation. The book raises issues of the morality of Yahweh himself. How could the Creator command the murder of all of these people?

Some have rationalized that since God creates, God can destroy. Yet the obscenity of the carnage painted in this divinely inspired book of the Bible should test the moral sensitivity of those who love God and neighbor today.

The historical-critical scholar, therefore, might question the veracity of these stories. The biblical archeologist might want to verify sites and villages that are listed in the Book of Joshua. Much of this work has been done and more will continue to be.

On the one hand, some historical-critical scholars have promulgated an hypothesis which runs quite contrary to the biblical account.

> *That the story of Moses as recounted in the Pentateuch is a late literary construction is supported by a recent and increasingly accepted hypothesis put forward on other grounds, that there was no mass immigration of Israel into Canaan from outside at all! George E. Mendenhnll and Norman K. Gottwald were the first to cast doubt on the historical credibility of the migration from Egypt to Canaan, and on the role of Moses in such a movement. Their view has been supported on both archaeological and sociological grounds. These scholars and those who have followed them maintain that there was no occupation of the land from outside. Rather, the later Israelites were actually descendants of part of the Canaanite population which, whether individually or in a corporate revolutionary movement, had detached itself from the life of the Canaanite cities of the plains with their surrounding agricultural territories, and had gradually established itself in the previously uninhabited, or sparsely inhabited, hill country. There was no "conquest" of Canaan by immigrants...* (Whybray, ibid, 67)

On the other hand, according to the OHBW, there are three scholarly hypotheses which have been advanced to account for the emergence of Israel in the Promised Land.

1. **The Conquest Hypothesis**—This view agrees, for the most part, with the biblical narrative in Joshua. This hypothesis is not accepted by most historical-critical scholars.

2. **The Pastoral Nomad Hypothesis**—Early Israel evolved from pastoral tent-dwelling nomadic groups to agriculturally stationary tribes. Israeli archaeologist Israel Finkelstein has updated the hypothesis, but this, too, is not accepted by most scholars.

3. **The Peasants' Revolt Hypothesis**—According to this view, the Israelites consisted of oppressed Canaanite peasants who revolted against city-state control and found freedom, and religion, in the countryside. This hypothesis has its modern-day scholarly supporters.

So, what is the adherent of the historical-critical method to make of the inspired book Joshua? One of the most convincing hypotheses comes from Old Testament scholar, Anthony Ceresko. Called the **Moses' Group Hypothesis** by some, today scholars realize that Israel was actually formed by a loose federation of tribes that wandered into the desolate hill country to avoid the oppressive government and social strata found in the surrounding land of Canaan. Whether they wanted to or not, these tribes were often forced to assist each other in order to survive, both through sharing resources and in banding together for protection from invaders. It is most likely that a group of slaves who managed to escape from Egypt eventually found their way to the hill country that has become Israel, and eventually merged their story of escape with the other tribes of Israel, comprised mostly of former Canaanites. "One of the components that went into the creation of Israel was the Moses group or Exodus group," writes Ceresko, "The present shape of their story of rescue from Egypt identifies this group as *Israel*. The Moses group was *not* Israel. Israel came into being *only later* in the hill country of Canaan. The great majority of those who eventually became Israel were indigenous and diverse groups of *Canaanites*, each of which brought separate experiences and separate stories to what eventually would be woven into a single common fabric."

A note about Anthony Ceresko: A Catholic priest and biblical scholar who has an excellent article on the Book of Jonah in the JBC, Anthony Ceresko (1942–2005) has given us an eye-opening account of Israel's origins and development, and of the complex scriptures that shaped that development. An advocate of the Documentary Hypothesis, or Four source theory (J, E, D, P) he grounds his approach in Norman Gottwald's revolutionary thesis on Israel's origins. Arguing against reading the early historical books as straightforward history, Gottwald (and in his turn Ceresko) show how these texts emerged as the self-defining narrative of a loose confederation of marginalized Canaanite hill tribes and refugees. The function of these texts, in other words, was to bind the tribes and create the ideological basis for the continued existence of this special confederacy.

As to the "morality" issue in the narrative in Joshua, the JBC sees an evolution of morality in biblical writings.

> *The morality of the OT shows both* **growth** *and* **limitations**. *At the beginning of the growth, the historical books from Gen. through Kgs., show Israelite heroes and heroines frequently acting on a low moral level...The* **limitations** *of Israelite morality have often been pointed out; they include the acceptance of slavery, polygamy, and divorce, the double standard of sexual morality..., a remarkably intense hatred of foreigners, inhumanity in war, and a certain laxness in regard to mendacity and theft. In these instances Israelite morality fails to rise entirely above that of its world...*(JBC 123).

Moral **growth** is seen in the Wisdom literature, although there are many references to the need for Yahweh to avenge one's enemies, most notably in Psalms.

By inference, then, does the JBC, and thus, the view of many Catholic historical-critical scholars, accept the "conquest hypothesis"? The Pontifical Biblical Commission of 1909 decreed the historicity of the primitive narrative of Genesis 1– 3; *a fortiori* it would seem from this document the Church does not tolerate that a Catholic deny the historicity of Joshua.

However, The Pontifical Biblical Commission's 1909 view, as well as those decrees issued between 1905 and 1915 now have little more than historic interest, being implicitly revoked by later decrees and by Vatican II. (JBC 72: 25)

The JBC, with full ecclesiastical approval within the Catholic community, states in 7: 9:

> *The depiction of a total Israelite conquest is a retroversion to the premonarchical period of a political fact of the monarch. Inner-biblical evidence frequently contradicts the picture of total annihilation of the inhabitants of the land...Archaeological evidence confirms the literary analysis of the book: few if any of the major episodes in Joshua can be shown to be historical. Thus, neither Jericho nor Ai nor Gibeon was occupied in the period in which most scholars would date the emergence of Israel in Canaan (ca. 1200 BC)...For the most part, then, the archaeological record contradicts the narrative.*

So, what is the historical-critical adherent to believe about the Book of Joshua? Accepting the fact that the book is divinely inspired, one might see in it a continuation of salvation history (not in the conventional sense of historical accuracy) begun in Genesis, wherein the revelation of God to his chosen people is further advanced. Yahweh delivers on his covenantal promises to Abraham and Moses by his restoration of the Promised Land to his people, but not in the manner described in the Book of Joshua.

16

The Growth of Yahwism

The Pentateuch assumes, from the beginning, that God, or Yahweh, or Elohim, after the sin of Adam and Eve, selected a people for himself through which he would reveal himself. In Vatican II's *Dei Verbum*, Chapter IV, Sec. 14, we read:

> *In carefully planning and preparing the salvation of the whole human race the God of infinite love, by a special dispensation, chose for Himself a people to whom He would entrust His promises. First He entered into a covenant with Abraham (see Gen. 15:18) and, through Moses, with the people of Israel (see Ex. 24:8). To this people which He had acquired for Himself, He so manifested Himself through words and deeds as the one true and living God that Israel came to know by experience the ways of God with men.*

Yet one has to wonder how much of this favored selection was known by those who followed Moses, much less those descendants of Abraham hundreds of years before.

Despite Egypt's brief official embrace of monotheism during the reign of the Pharaoh Akhenaten in the 1300s BC, the future Israelites in sojourn in Egypt had little knowledge of, or contact with, monotheism until the Mosaic era.

The Documentary Hypothesis demonstrates the possibility that in the last 1000 years before the birth of Jesus Christ, there was a growing awareness of this selection by Yahweh, particularly as the canon of Jewish scripture was developed. The Great Exile to Babylon (586–537 BC) saw the final redaction of the Torah. However, the redactors were dealing with accumulated material that cannot have had a long shelf life. On page 16, in my book *The Evolution of Belief in the Afterlife in the Old Testament*, I ask the question:

> *What, then, are the earliest writings in the Old Testament?* The Song of Deborah *(Judges 5: 1–31) and the* Testament of Jacob (Genesis 49: 1–27) *are certainly among the leading candidates. In its present form, the* Testament of Jacob *dates back to the kingship of David (1000 – 962 BC) and the* Song of Deborah *at least to the time of the Judges (1200–1050 BC). The* Song of Deborah *is an example of the earliest Hebrew poetry, and some of its verses are still obscure.*

How aware, then, were the Israelites of their dependence on a monotheistic deity prior to Moses? It would seem that if they did not even know Yahweh's name until Moses learned it, their religion was not what we today called "Yahwism," or belief in Yahweh.

In the patriarchal period (2000–1700 BC) which began with Abraham, God is unnamed, although referred to in Genesis as "the God of Abraham, Isaac, and Jacob." Since the Torah was written in the next millennium, the names that appear, such as *elohim* or *olam* (eternal), are anachronistic. Almost a millennium passed before Yahwism came into the religious awareness of the primal groups which later were called Israel.

Yahweh was the personal name of Israel's God. What the name signifies is uncertain, although Exodus 3: 13–14 has been translated in various ways as "I am who am," or "I am the one who causes existence," "I am existence," and others. The

meaning, therefore, of *Yahweh,* may have even been unclear
to most of the Israelites, and, despite the initial use of the
Hebrew consonants YHWH, when vowels were added later,
the vowel name *Adonai* was used instead out of respect for the
sacred name. (In interfaith Jewish / Christian seminars, etc., if
Christians incorporate hymns such as "Yahweh, I know you are
near," Jewish participants may sing *Adonai*...or simply remain
silent.)

Several scholars have written about the religion of Israel
from its beginnings to the Christian era. J.C. De Moor, in
The Rise of Yahwism: The Roots of Israelite Monotheism,
Leuven: Peeters, 1990, sees Yahwism as a rejection of a highly
devalued polytheism. Mark S. Smith, in *The Origins of Biblical
Monotheism: Israel's Polytheistic Background and the Ugaritic
Texts,* Oxford University Press, 2001, maintains that polytheism
existed in ancient Israel. *El* (plural *elohim*) may have been
the original deity worshiped by Israelites and associated with
the Exodus, but Yahweh emerged and absorbed *El.* Mitchell
Dahood, S.J., contends in his series on the Psalms that the
composition of several of the psalms is better understood from
the study of Ugaritic poetry.

So far we have been following the path forged by Wellhausen
and the Documentary Hypothesis. Robert Brow, in the chapter
"Origins of Religion," found in *Eerdman's Handbook to the
World's Religions,* Eerdman Publishing, 1994, maintains that
Wellhausen, because of Darwin's influence, was supportive of
the hypothesis that religion began with animism, progressed to
polytheism, and then evolved into monotheism:

> *Wellhausen's reconstruction has now, however,
> been discredited. And we also have examples of
> monotheism and elaborate priestly religion from
> long before the time of Abraham. The theory of
> the upward evolution of religion is therefore being*

restated to push the emergence of monotheism back into the shadows of prehistory. Led by Wilhelm Schmidt of Vienna, anthropologists have shown that the religion of the hundreds of isolated tribes in the world today is not primitive in the sense of being original. The tribes have a memory of a 'high god', a benign creator-father-god, who is no longer worshipped because that god is not feared. Instead of offering sacrifice, they concern themselves with the pressing problems of how to appease the vicious spirits of the jungle. The threats of the medicine man are more strident than the still, small voice of the father-god.

We see, then, that the evolution of religion from animism can no longer be assumed as axiomatic and that some anthropologists now suggest that monotheism may be more naturally primitive as a world-view than animism. Their research suggests that tribes are not animistic because they have continued unchanged since the dawn of history. Rather, the evidence indicates degeneration from a true knowledge of God.

Obviously, Brow's view leans toward fundamentalism. However, his observations are worth noting. Nevertheless, the majority of historical-critical scholars still hold Wellhausen's work as fundamental to understanding the origins of the Torah.

17

Nonbiblical History Merges with the Biblical Narrative

Biblical scholars point to King David as the first person in the Bible that has a corroborative nonbiblical resource backing up his existence. Two inscriptions from the 800s BC may point to an Israelite monarchy. Recently, in northern Israel, an Aramaic inscription was found at Tel Dan refers to the "the king of Israel," and "the house of David." The first inscription, found in 1868, in Moab, known as the Mesha Stela, while referring specifically to Omri as "king of Israel," infers the existence of the "house of David."

The biblical account of the period of Samuel, the last of the judges, and the early monarchies of Saul, David, and Solomon do contain some authentic political, economic, and topographic detail. However, archeological discoveries have not yielded an overwhelming amount of corroborative authentication of the monarchies. (OHBW: 233, 234)

However, the biblical account of the early monarchy, despite the consensus among most historical-critical scholars that there are stories of royal hyperbole in the biblical narrative, marks the beginning of the merging of the biblical narrative with nonbiblical history.

An often used illustration of this merging comes in the form of two accounts of the same battle for Jerusalem in 701 BC, one from the nonbiblical account given by the Assyrian King Sennecherib (705–681 BC), and the other, the biblical accounts, found in 2 Kings and 2 Chronicles.

First, Sennecherib's account:

> *As to Hezekiah, the Jew, he did not submit to my yoke, I laid siege to his strong cities, walled forts, and countless small villages, and conquered them by means of well-stamped earth-ramps and battering-rams brought near the walls with an attack by foot soldiers, using mines, breeches as well as trenches. I drove out 200,150 people, young and old, male and female, horses, mules, donkeys, camels, big and small cattle beyond counting, and considered them slaves. Himself I made a prisoner in Jerusalem, his royal residence, like a bird in a cage. I surrounded him with earthwork in order to molest those who were his city's gate. Thus I reduced his country, but I still increased the tribute and the presents to me as overlord which I imposed upon him beyond the former tribute, to be delivered annually. Hezekiah himself, did send me, later, to Nineveh, my lordly city, together with 30 talents of gold, 800 talents of silver, precious stones, antimony, large cuts of red stone, couches inlaid with ivory, nimedu-chairs inlaid with ivory, elephant-hides, ebony-wood, boxwood and all kinds of valuable treasures, his own daughters and concubines...(ANET, 288)*

Then, the biblical account in 2 Kings: 18, 19:

> *In the fourteenth year of King Hezekiah, Sennacherib, king of Assyria, went on an expedition against all the fortified cities of Judah and captured them.*

Hezekiah, king of Judah, sent this message to the king of Assyria at Lachish: "I have done wrong. Leave me, and I will pay whatever tribute you impose on me." The king of Assyria exacted three hundred talents of silver and thirty talents of gold from Hezekiah, king of Judah. Hezekiah paid him all the funds there were in the temple of the Lord and in the palace treasuries...That night the angel of the Lord went forth and struck down 185,000 men in the Assyrian camp. Early the next morning, there they were, all the corpses of the dead. So Sennacherib, the king of Assyria, broke camp and went back home to Nineveh. When he was worshiping in the temple of his god Nisroch, his sons Adram-melech and Sharezer slew him with the sword and fled into the land of Ararat. (NAB: 2 Kings: 18–19)

The results are similar...Hezekiah's Jerusalem was not taken, due, in part, to his construction of a lengthy water tunnel, a third of a mile long, mostly less than three feet wide, and, in a few places, less than five feet in height, which winds from the Gihon Spring to the Pool of Siloam. However, it is a good example of ancient "spin" in ancient history.

18

The Psalms of David... Further Historical Evidence?

I remember my shock, not much more than a decade ago, upon hearing Fr. Paul Kreimes, teacher of Hebrew and Old Testament courses of Detroit Sacred Heart Major Seminary, in his course on the Psalms, announce that none of the psalms in the Book of Psalms have been proven definitively to have been written by King David. That was his observation despite the fact that seventy-three psalms have in or as their superscription *leDawid*, usually translated "of [by] David." The preposition has a large number of meanings, but its most common translations are "to, for, of." It is used for psalms attributed to others as well. Many of the psalms begin with a superscription that has traditionally been understood to attribute authorship to the passage. However, critical scholarship generally rejects the reliability of these notations.

The claim in Jewish and Christian sacred books to authorship by famous figures who did not write them is demonstrable. Pseudonymity, or using a false name, is found in several cases in the Old and New Testament. Solomon did not write Ecclesiastes or Wisdom, just as Paul did not write Hebrews.

To say, however, that none of the Psalms were written by David is not what Kreimes taught...just that the Davidic authorship of the Psalms is in question.

As a matter of fact, the origin of the Psalms has been the topic of much scholarly work. Certainly one of the scholars that has had a tremendous impact on the subject of biblical authorship is Mitchell Dahood, referred to above. His contention that several of the Psalms find linguistic similarities to the literature of the Ugaritic culture is still of great interest today.

Knowledge of the ancient Canaanite city-state of Ugarit is a necessity for those studying the Old Testament. The literature of the city and its theology help us understand the meaning of various Biblical passages as well as aiding us in deciphering difficult Hebrew words. Ugarit was at its political, religious and economic height around the 12th century BC. In 1928 a group of French archaeologists discovered at Ras Shamra, a few kilometers east of the Mediterranean coast of Syria, a collection of tablets carved with an unknown cuneiform script. In 1932 the identification of the site was made when some of the tablets were deciphered; the city was the ancient and famous site of Ugarit.

Dahood has been both criticized and praised for his advancement of the position that the ancient language of Ugarit, and its sacred literature, played a significant role in the formation of both the Psalms and Proverbs. In the Introduction to his volume III on the Psalms, his assessment of his role is telling:

> *The lively critical reaction to Psalms I, 1–50 and Psalms II, 51–100 (AB, vols. 16 and 17) belies the apologetic dictum of Saint Jerome that of all the gifts or graces bestowed by Heaven, that of the translator ranks lowest in the scale of importance. Modern scholars know better; they realize that the soundness of biblical theology and anthropology depends upon the soundness of the translation on which these disciplines are based. Try as we will, we cannot escape words, in themselves, or the subtle*

grammatical structures that build up sentences and paragraphs.

Let us cut to the chase: Were the Psalms influenced by pagan hymns? Another way of putting the question…Were the Psalms, in some cases, reworked Ugaritic hymns to pagan gods?

Anglican biblical scholar Allen Ross notes in an online article to be found at http://www.bible.org/page.php?page_id=2749 that:

> *The important point…is that the Israelites were not isolated from their world, and their literature, especially the psalms, was not written without knowledge of reference to the views of the world. The language and the images that are used may seem at times perplexing to us, but they would have been clear to them. The more we learn of their world, the better we will understand the fine points of their literature, our Book of Psalms.*

However, Ross maintains that, although there are allusions to major motifs of mythology, they are subtle in the Psalms. The modern reader may not pick up on this, but to the Israelite living in the midst of pagans they would be clear. Because these ideas were a threat to Israel, Ross observes, it is probably not likely that they were borrowed and blended into Yahwism.

So, were the psalms influenced by pagan cultures? Yes. However, the number of them remains an open question, since many of the psalms can be dated to exilic or post-exilic years. Did David compose some of the psalms? Probably. Scholars simply do not know. Even Dahood maintained that no psalms have been identified with the Ras Shamra texts discovered at Ugarit. However, there are more scholars now that would grant that some of the psalms were composed in the period when the Davidic monarchy is thought to have occurred, around 1000 BC.

19

Tobit, Judith, and Esther

The Protestant canon of the Old Testament excludes Tobit and Judith. Esther is in the Protestant Canon. The Catholic and Orthodox canons include all three. The Jewish canon omits Tobit, and places Judith and Esther in a grouping called the Writings (Simply stated, Jewish canons refer to the Law, the Prophets, and the Writings.)

As to the historical value of the three books, there is little. Tobit is an example of Hebrew romantic writing, with its composition dated as late as 180 BC. It contains historical inaccuracies as well as manipulation of "history" as regards its characters.

Judith is didactic fiction, complete with many historical inaccuracies, probably composed less than a century before Christ's birth by an unknown author.

Esther, composed in the 400s BC, is quite probably another example of historical fiction, although details about the Persian Empire are quite accurate, and it "may reflect remembrances of a real or threatened pogrom against the Jews in the Persian Empire or even an historical Mordecai and Esther with influence at the Persian court...however, the story as it now exists is a fictional narrative..." (JBC 38: 52)

How are historical-critical scholars able to come to the conclusion that these books are basically fiction?

The answer, particularly as regards Tobit and Judith, is its inaccurate reporting of the history surrounding the stories as well as the content of the books which are obviously contrived stories of authors who focused on Yahweh's love of Israel, especially in hopeless situations.

The memorable story in the Book of Tobit is an entertaining one that is filled with coincidental improbabilities. Ross TenEyck made the story of two of the protagonists, Tobias (son of Tobit) and Esther, into a children's play. In his introduction he lightheartedly summarizes the story:

> Tobit is blind, because birds pooped in his eyes. Also, he's lost all his money as a penalty for keeping to the strict Jewish Law, despite the commands of the Assyrians. He bewails his lot and prays for God to strike him dead.
>
> Meanwhile, Sarah is upset because she has had seven husbands, each one of whom has been killed on their wedding night by the demon Asmodeus; and it's getting hard to find new fiancées. She bewails her lot and prays for God to strike her dead. God hears both these prayers, and sends the angel Raphael to straighten things out.
>
> Meanwhile, Tobit suddenly remembers some money that he gave to a friend of his long ago to safeguard. He decides to send his son, Tobias, to fetch it; if only they can find a guide who knows the way to the city where his friend lives. Lo and behold, a providential stranger appears at the front door—Raphael, of course—who happens to know the way. He agrees to guide Tobias. Along the way, Tobias catches a fish when it tries to swallow his foot. Raphael advises him to save the heart, liver, and gall bladder of the fish. Burning the heart and liver will cure a person

who is being afflicted by a demon—just in case Tobias happens to run into such a person—while the gall bladder will cure blindness.

Tobias and Raphael stop to spend the night at the house of Raguel and Sarah. It comes out that Sarah and Tobias are related in such a way that the Law says they must marry. Tobias is willing, although Sarah tries to suggest that it might be a better idea to leave well enough alone. Nevertheless, they are married; and that night, Tobias burns the heart and liver, which sends Asmodeus screaming into the night, where Raphael administers a little smackdown. Meanwhile, Raguel digs a grave, so as to be able to get rid of the body early, before the neighbors notice. Much to his—and everyone's— surprise, Tobias comes down for breakfast in the morning.

Raphael is sent off to fetch the money held by Tobit's friend; and then the whole party heads back home to Nineveh. Tobit's blindness is cured by the gall bladder; and between the money from his friend, and Sarah's dowry, Tobit's fortunes are restored. Everyone lives happily ever after. http://alumnus. caltech.edu/~teneyck/liturgy/tobit.html

Historically, the Book of Tobit had its doubters as to its canonicity. St. Jerome omitted it from his list. Sts. Augustine and Ambrose, however, maintained it was canonical. Luther, in agreement with Jerome, omitted it; however, the book was considered divinely inspired in the Catholic canon as far back as the Council of Hippo (393 AD) and earned final deuterocanonical status in the Council of Trent in the 16th century.

Tobit, despite its fictional nature, teaches important lessons.

Suffering is a test, not necessarily a punishment. God rewards the just for their trust in Him. God is merciful and free.

The Book of Judith (the name means "Jewish woman") brings into Scripture a heroine, surprising for its inclusion in a generally male-dominated list of national "deliverers." The book begins with an historical setting that fits with non-biblical history. It is in the reign of Nebuchadnezzar (ruler from 605–562 BC), the most famous of the Neo-Babylonian kings, that the southern kingdom with its capital Jerusalem fell to begin the Great Exile in 587 BC.

The story of Judith involves the trust of a woman that Yahweh would deliver the Israelites from Nebuchadnezzar's general, Holofernes. According to the book, Holofernes was ordered in 593 BC to wreak vengeance on the nations of the west that had withheld their assistance to his reign. The Jewish inhabitants of Bethulia, commonly believed to be Meselieh, after a month without water, lose faith and are ready to surrender. Judith, a beautiful widow, promises the people that if they wait five more days, Yahweh will deliver them. She presents herself to Holofernes as a seductress, with a deceptive plan as to how to defeat her people. The general is captivated by her and desires intercourse. Having fallen into a drunken stupor, Holofernes is killed by Judith with his own sword. Judith cuts off his head, puts it in her bag, and leaves the soldiers' camp. Judith returns to Bethulia, where she receives a hero's welcome. She outlines a plan of attack which is successful. After the victory, Judith was honored and sought after in marriage. She remained a widow, living to the age of 105. The book closes with the statement: "During the life of Judith and for a long time after her death, no one again disturbed the Israelites." Obviously, the statement disagrees with history, since six years later, Jerusalem is destroyed by the Babylonians and the Great Exile begins.

The Book of Esther tells the story of an even more famous

Jewish heroine. In this post-exilic story, the King of Persia, Xerxes the Great (ruler from 485–465 BC), also known as Ahasuerus, is married to Queen Vashti. The queen refuses to appear before her husband and his cohort. Result? The Queen is out of a job, and the King looks for a new queen. The character Mordicai appears, who becomes an enemy of the King's prime minister, Haman for refusing to bow before Haman. Mordicai is secretly a Jew, as is his cousin, the beautiful Esther, who is chosen to be the King's new queen. Haman is described as a descendant of Agag, king of Amalek. (Haman has revenge on his mind against the Jews for not allowing any of the Amalekites to survive, but that is another story.) Haman persuades Xerxes (in the book, a persuadable sort of fellow, if not an outright simpleton) to issue a decree calling for the genocide of all Jews. However, the King does not know that Esther is Jewish. Esther saves the day for her people: at the risk of endangering her own safety, she warns Xerxes of Haman's plot to kill all the Jews. Haman and his sons are hanged on the gallows he had had built for Mordecai, and Mordecai becomes prime minister in Haman's place. However, for some unknown reason, Xerxes' edict decreeing the murder of the Jews cannot be rescinded, so he issues another edict allowing the Jews to take up arms and fight to kill their enemies, which they do. To this day, Jews celebrate the Esther story on the Feast of Purim with gift-giving, works of charity, recitation in public of the Book of Esther, and a meal of celebration of Jewish deliverance.

20

The Book of Jonah

A test of whether someone interprets the Old Testament literally is how the person views the Book of Jonah. The book has been variously dated by scholars from the 6th century to the early 3rd century BC, although the book itself implies an 8th century dating. However, scholars have dismissed the early dating.

Jesus references Jonah in Matthew 12: 38–42 and in Luke 11:29–32 and compares his own impending time to be spent in the grave to Jonah's 72 hour sojourn in the belly of a fish. This intertestamental reference would seem to end the discussion for the literalist as to the veracity of the Book of Jonah.

However, Jesus also limited his mission on earth to "the lost sheep of the house of Israel." (Matthew 10: 6; 15:24). These literal words of Jesus obviously run contrary to the universal salvific nature of Jesus' role in the redemption of all mankind.

Another instance of intriguing statements by Jesus is found in Luke 20: 37–38: "That the dead will rise even Moses made known in the passage about the bush, when he called 'Lord' the God of Abraham, the God of Isaac, and the God of Jacob; and he is not God of the dead, but of the living, for to him all are alive." This response was made to the Sadducees, who did not believe in the resurrection of the dead, and who had posed the question of which husband a childless woman, who had seven husbands all of whom died, would have upon her death.

The belief in the afterlife came slowly in the millennium

following Moses, and certainly was not reflected in many Jewish writings until the post-exilic period, so the literal value of Jesus' words are questionable, and open to critical analysis.

Intertestamental, as well as intratestamental explanations may reflect the gospel author's own view or that of the oral tradition from which he came. Jesus also used knowledge that, in his human nature, he would have been taught or what his audience may have been familiar with.

Back to the Book of Jonah...The two-page "book" relates how the prophet was called by God to preach to the great city of Nineveh because of its wickedness. The prophet runs away, boards a ship, a storm comes up, and he is thrown overboard. A great fish swallows him, keeping him in its belly for three days, then spews him out on land. Reluctantly, the prophet journeys to Nineveh, the capital city of Assyria, where the city and its ruler repent of their wickedness. The prophet is miffed that God deals mercifully with such an evil bunch of people, but God reminds him that he cares for the city.

To view the Book of Jonah from a fundamentalist point of view, Rev. John Schultz, a 37 year veteran Belgian missionary to New Guinea, notes the following:

> *Higher Criticism sees in the book nothing more than a legend, written by an anonymous author before the second century, and who chose the historical Jonah, who lived centuries earlier, as the hero of his story.*
>
> *The basis for their supposition is, in the first place, the miracle with the fish, and the thought that some words in the book would date from a later period. How such a thesis can be scientifically established is not clear. To consider this book as anything but a historical document would be contrary to our concept of the inspiration of the Bible as the Word*

of God. One can only place Jonah in the category of fables if one starts out with the prejudice that miracles, such as described in this story, are impossible. The question remains if miracles in the physical sense of the word occur. The greatest manifestation of supernatural power is the mass conversion of the inhabitants of Nineveh. (http:// www.biblecommentaries.com/source/johnschultz/ BC_Jonah.pdf)

However, for most historical-critical scholars, it would be a stretch to find anything of historical value in the Book of Jonah. There are glaring improbabilities...Jonah being swallowed by a fish for three days...Nineveh was in no mood for repentance, having become the capital city of Assyria under Sennecherib (Chapter XVII) who destroyed tens of villages in his march to Hezekiah's Jerusalem in 701BC...yet, Nineveh repented. That there was a Jonah during the reign of Jeroboam II (786– 746 BC) is mentioned in 2 Kings: 14–25, so obviously the "repentance" did not last long! The author of the Book of Jonah most probably used the Jonah of 2 Kings to give the story an historical basis. Assyria had long been a feared empire in Jewish history, committing atrocities against the Israelites on more than one occasion. There is no historical evidence from non-biblical sources, that Nineveh ever repented of anything, much less take suggestions from a Jewish prophet.

So, to the historical-critical scholar, what is this two-page treatise all about? The real miracle of the "book" is that it made it into the Jewish canon at all. The Jewish people were Yahweh's chosen. That redemption of one of Israel's worst enemies would be possible and that Yahweh cared for non-Jews was not in the Jewish mindset. That is the miracle. The story is a parable, a fictional never-to-be-forgotten story of a reluctant prophet, a great fish, and the conversion of an enemy's capital city.

21

The Book of Ruth

Although the Book of Ruth is listed almost immediately after the Torah in the Christian Old Testament, its theme is similar to the Book of Jonah, in that non-Jews, if they followed Yahweh's laws, were loved by Yahweh. It appears in the Writings *(ketubim)* of the Jewish canon, and was considered an historical book for centuries. It hardly deserves the title "book," since, like the Book of Jonah, it is extremely brief…only three pages in length.

Today, however, the work, while historically possible, is for most historical-critical scholars a work of fiction.

The events in Ruth purportedly occur "while the judges are judging," so it is placed immediately after the Book of Judges in the Old Testament. As a matter of fact, Ruth is thought to have been part of the Book of Judges.

There are several parts to the story of Ruth that are interesting. One is the reference to Bethlehem of Judah as the point of origin of the story; another is the famous quote of the widow Ruth to her widowed mother-in-law Naomi when Naomi urged Ruth and Ruth's also widowed sister-in-law Orpah (both were non-Jewish Moabites who had married Naomi's sons), "…wherever you go I will go, wherever you lodge I will lodge. Your people shall be my people, and your God my God." Another point of interest is the acceptance of the non-Jew Ruth into the Jewish community, which was to run contrary to the post-exilic call of Ezra in chapter 9: 12 of the Book of Ezra: "Do not, then, give your daughters to their (non-Jews) sons, and do not take their daughters for your sons..." (NAB: Ezra: 9: 12)

This attempt to keep the Jewish people free of intermarriage, and thus the influences of other religions, has led to a strange situation in the current Israeli government. Israel, like Canada and New Zealand, has no written constitution in one single document, but rather a number of Basic Laws. In order to be Prime Minister of Israel, for example, one has to be chosen by the 120-member Knesset (or legislative body). To be a member of the Knesset, one has to be an Israeli national. *(Israel—Basic Law: The Knesset, Sec. 6)*

While ancient religious law is not the basis of Israel's Basic Laws, it is clear that the government of modern Israel is to be in the hands of Jewish nationals. To this day, non-Jews in Israel's government are few and far between.

The Book of Ruth is probably most well known for the purported genealogy of David. The widow Ruth, returning to Bethlehem, was urged by her mother-in-law to make herself available to the relative Boaz. Ruth and Boaz married and bore Obed, who became the father of Jesse, who was the father of David.

22

The Historical Books of Kings

David is a pivotal person in both Jewish and Christian traditions. For Jews, David is the person who galvanized the Jewish nation into a formidable religious and political power. For Christians, he is the ancestor prophesied to be the forebear of Jesus Christ.

The nomenclature of the Books of Kings has different meanings. There are four books in the Old Testament that are in question here. In the *Vulgate* of St. Jerome both titles are given, i.e., 1 Samuel is also called 1 Kings. To avoid confusion, Catholic writers list the "king" books as: 1 Samuel and 2 Samuel followed by 1 Kings and 2 Kings. In the KJV the "kings" books are 1, 2, 3 and 4 Kings. The NIV and other translations follow the Catholic listing.

For our purposes, we will examine the historicity of 1 and 2 Kings in the NIV listing. Comment has been previously made that 1 and 2 Samuel contain instances of royal hyperbole, and while their historicity has spurred a tremendous amount of research, there was general agreement that these books, as well as the first eleven chapters of 1 Kings were deemed of great historical value. However, according to the OHBW:

> *More recently, the traditional assessment of 1 and 2 Samuel and 1 Kings 1–11 as reliable sources for understanding monarchic history has been turned on its head...well before the advent of these newer*

literary analyses, scholars recognized that the dramatic tales of Samuel and Saul, and of David and Solomon, are embedded in the so-called Deuteronomic History (DH)...The information about the material world of the early monarchy...is sometimes viewed as hopelessly exaggerated if not outright fictive.

Recent archaeological surveys, for example, do confirm the historical value of topographical details and place-names in the narratives of 1 and 2 Samuel, and they indicate that sites newly founded in the late eleventh and early tenth centuries correspond with places mentioned in the Samuel narratives, particularly with David.

(However,) given the extent and grandeur of the early monarchy as depicted in biblical writings, it is striking that absolutely no references to Saul, David, Solomon, or the new Israelite kingdom appear in any ancient Near Eastern documents of the late eleventh or tenth century BC. (OHBW: 226–232)

The basic outlines of 1 and 2 Kings are, by contrast, generally considered historical with certain caveats. The names and order of the kings, the split of Israel into two kingdoms after Solomon *circa* 920 BC, the Northern Kingdom (called thereafter the Kingdom of Israel) and the Southern Kingdom (called later the Kingdom of Judah), and the Great Exile (587 BC) give Jewish history from the viewpoint of the writer(s) of the Deuteronomic History (DH). We have already noted the corroborative merging of non-biblical history with the Bible in the Sennecherib-Hezekiah battle.

However, the DH chronicler is less interested in accurately recording events than in explaining the tragic history of

Yahweh's people. The sources that the DH compiler used...
*The Acts of Solomon, The Chronicles of the Kings of Judah,
and the Chronicles of the Kings of Israel*...are now lost.

23

The Book of Job

The Book of Job deals with one of the most difficult questions in life. Why does God allow good people to suffer? It is concerned, also, with a common perception prevalent in Jewish thought...namely, that wealth, power, a good name, and the best of family and friends are Yahweh's reward in this life for faithfulness to Him and his law.

The book turns that common perception upside down. Job is a good man, blessed with friends, family, and many possessions. Yet he finds himself sitting in ashes, his body covered entirely with severe boils, with his wife berating him and accusing him of being stubborn and refusing to admit guilt for an unknown sin...all this after Job loses all of his wealth in sheep, camels, oxen, and work animals...possessions greater than those of any of the men of the East...and, to top it off, all of his ten children are killed when the house they were partying at collapses from a great wind.

Enter his friends. Upon hearing of Job's misfortunes, three of his friends come to offer sympathy and comfort. However, their amazement at his condition is so great, they remain speechless in his presence for seven days and nights.

Then begins a series of three cycles of speeches, with responses by Job, wherein his friends hammer home the point his wife had made: "Job, you wouldn't be suffering this way if you had been faithful to God."

Job protests his innocence, but his friends are not convinced. After the three-fold cycle of speeches, Job concludes with a moving plea for understanding. He lists his life's good deeds, along with disclaimers as to having done anything evil. Not content to let Job have the last word, Elihu, presumably the wisest of the three friends, sums up the situation, laying blame once again on Job.

After this last tirade against Job, God speaks. Instead of answering the question of why Job is suffering so, God asks a series of questions of Job.

They center on the issue of who really controls the universe and knows how it was formed, how it operates, how the laws of nature work, where the rain and ice come from...What about the birth of mountain goats, the horse's strength, the flight of the eagle? God presses the issue that He alone is sovereign over all that is, leaving Job finally to concede that God can do all things, that as a human, Job does not understand how God can be all-knowing and all-powerful. God then scolds Job's friends and rewards Job with "twice as much as he had before." (NAB: Job 42:10)

What is the historical-critical scholar to make of this divinely-inspired masterpiece of literature?

If the reader of this book cannot answer the question, welcome to the club. It is obvious that the Book of Job is didactic fiction, based on everyone's experience with good and evil. However, the central question of why do the good suffer is left unanswered. God does not explain his reasons for allowing misfortune to strike the innocent. The author does a marvelous job of posing a humanly unanswerable question and leaves the reader with no resolution to it.

The author is unknown and the text is extremely difficult to translate. Since there are no historical allusions in the work, it is also difficult to date. The Book of Job is thought by some to have been a postexilic work, but at present the date of composition is open to question.

24

"The Writings" and The Wisdom Literature of Other Cultures

"Wisdom" literature is found in many ancient cultures and there are striking similarities with that body of writing and the "wisdom" literature found in the Bible. This biblical literature, called "The Writings" or *kituvim*, in the Jewish listing includes Psalms, Proverbs, Job, Song of Songs (Song of Solomon), Ruth, Lamentations, Ecclesiastes, Esther, Daniel, Ezra-Nehemiah, and Chronicles.

The "good man who suffers" which we find in Job is found in Sumerian and Babylonian texts. In a Sumerian work, *Man and his God* (ANET, 589–591), we read a similar theme. The Book of Psalms has several psalms of lament which echoes the dialogue below. The Sumerian writing predates all three biblical books, and reflects the concern of the author about the problem of the suffering, righteous person.

> *You have doled out to me suffering ever anew,*
> *I entered the house, heavy is the spirit,*
> *I, the young man, went out to the street, oppressed*
> *is the heart,*
> *With me, the valiant, my righteous shepherd has*
> *become angry...*
> *My companion says not a true word to me,*

My friend gives the lie to my righteous word.
The man of deceit has conspired against me,
(And) you, my god, do not thwart him,
You carry off my understanding,
The wicked has conspired against me
Angered you, stormed about, planned evil.
I, the wise, why am I bound to the ignorant youths?
I, the discerning, why am I counted among the
ignorant?
Food is all about, (yet) my food is hunger,
On the day shares were allotted to all, my allotted
share was suffering. (ANET, 590)

A similar poem, dating to around 1000 BC, comes from the Akkadian work, *The Dialogue about Human Misery* (ANET, 601–604). Like the dialogue in the Book of Job, there are protestations of innocence by the sufferer, followed by advice of friends similar to the friends of Job.

Sufferer:
Where is the counselor to whom I can relate my
trouble?
I am finished. Anguish has come upon me...

Friend:
Respected friend, what you say is sad.
Dear friend, you have let your mind dwell on evil.
You have made your good sense like that of an
incompetent person;
You have changed your beaming face to scowls...
He who looks to his god has a protective spirit;
The humble man who fears his goddess accumulates
wealth.

Sufferer:
My friend, your mind is a spring whose depth has
not been found,

The high swell of the sea, which does not subside.
I will ask you a question; listen to what I say.
Pay attention for a moment; hear my words...
My success has vanished, my stability has gone.
My strength is weakened, my prosperity has ended.
(ANET, 602)

While the similarities between these two examples are obvious, the format of *The Dialogue about Human Misery* matches that of the Book of Job. Again, the question for the historical-critical scholar is "Was the Book of Job based on the Babylonian poem?"

Always, there are differences between biblical and non-biblical works, particularly as regards the meanings of "god." Also, the message and conclusion of the biblical works often differ from non-biblical ones. However, the similarities are uncanny, and it is more than probable that the divinely-inspired author(s) of Job borrowed from similar pagan source material such as the above two examples.

The Book of Ecclesiastes dates from the postexilic period. Although the author names himself as the son of David, *Qoheleth, king in Jerusalem*, the name's meaning is unknown. David's most famous son was Solomon, and it was traditionally thought that Qoheleth was Solomon. However, as we have seen, historical-critical scholars have pointed out that the use of famous personages' names (pseudonymity) as authors gave credibility to the work, so it is believed that this practice is used here.

Perhaps the most famous passage of the book is contained in the first eight verses of chapter three:

> *There is an appointed time for everything, and a time for every affair under the heavens. A time to be born, and a time to die; a time to plant, and a time*

> *to uproot the plant. A time to kill, and a time to heal;*
> *a time to tear down, and a time to build. A time to*
> *weep, and a time to laugh; a time to mourn, and a*
> *time to dance. A time to scatter stones, and a time to*
> *gather them; a time to embrace, and a time to be far*
> *from embraces. A time to seek, and a time to lose; a*
> *time to keep, and a time to cast away. A time to rend,*
> *and a time to sew; a time to be silent, and a time*
> *to speak. A time to love, and a time to hate; a time*
> *of war, and a time of peace.* (NAB: Ecclesiastes, 3:
> 1–8)

The work represents an imperfect, worldly understanding of reality. Although the author believes in God, he does not believe in eternal life. The underlying theme is: *Enjoy the day, and do not go to extremes in the pursuit of happiness, because all is vanity, and all will end.* The term "vanity" (*hebel*) is used 37 times, and the work is constructed using an elaborate numerical plan. Ecclesiastes is written as a dialogue. The author talks to himself, so there is only one person, Qoheleth, who reflects to himself on a variety of topics.

The Dialogue of Pessimism, a short Akkadian dialogue, dated several hundred years before Ecclesiastes, between a master and his servant, is similar to the biblical work in its skepticism about the permanence of anything in this life. A series of intentions to do something...*get a chariot to drive to the palace...I intend to have children...I intend to make love to a woman...I will do something dishonest*...are given by the master. Each time the servant agrees, and each time the master changes his mind, citing the futility of where it gets him. Finally, the master orders suicide for himself and his servant as he asks the questions: *Who is so tall that he can reach to the heavens? Who is so broad that he can encompass the underworld?*

There are many other examples of extrabiblical wisdom

literature found in Egyptian and Greek cultures. Egyptian writings, such as the *Instruction of Ptahhotep* or the *Instruction of Amenemope* contain material similar to that in Proverbs. In the deuterocanonical works of Ecclesiasticus (Sirach) and the Wisdom of Solomon we see hints of Greek influence.

An excerpt from the *Instruction of Ptahhotep,* a papyrus book from the Fifth Dynasty of Egypt (3580 BC)

> *If you want a perfect conduct,*
> *To be free from every evil,*
> *Guard against the vice of greed:*
> *A grievous sickness without cure,*
> *There is no treatment for it.*
> *It embroils fathers, mothers,*
> *And the brothers of the mother,*
> *It parts wife from husband;*
> *It is a compound of all evils,*
> *A bundle of all hateful things.*
> *That man endures whose rule is rightness,*
> *Who walks a straight line;*
> *He will make a will by it,*
> *The greedy has no tomb...*
> *Be generous as long as you live,*
> *What leaves the storehouse does not return;*
> *It is the food to be shared which is coveted,*
> *One whose belly is empty is an accuser;*
> *One deprived becomes an opponent,*
> *Don't have him for a neighbor.*
> *Kindness is a man's memorial*
> *For the years after the action.*
> *Don't be proud of your knowledge,*
> *Consult the ignorant and the wise;*
> *The limits of art are not reached,*
> *No artist's skills are perfect;*
> *Good speech is more hidden than greenstone,*

Yet may be found among maids at the grindstones.

The work, like the Book of Proverbs, contains examples of the use of parallelism, both synonymous parallelism, which restates the idea of the first line in a different way, and synethetic parallelism, which expands upon what has been stated in the first line. While synonymous parallelism repeats what has been said in the first line, synethetic takes the thought of the first line farther—it develops the first thought further.

In the *Instruction of Ameneonope*, an Egyptian papyrus with 30 chapters of proverbs, written around 1200 BC, there are examples of virtually the same proverbs in both works:

Proverbs: Direct your ear and hear wise words. Set your heart to know them. For it is pleasant if you keep them in your inmost self. (22:17–18a)

Ameneonope: Give your ears and hear what is said, give your mind over to their interpretation: It is profitable to put them in your heart. (3,10)

....

Proverbs: Have I not written for you thirty counsels and teachings to teach you what is right and true? (22:20)

Ameneonope: Mark for your self these thirty chapters: They please, they instruct, they are the foremost of all books. (27,7)

....

Proverbs: Do not make friends with people prone to anger. With the hotheaded person do not associate. (22:24)

Ameneonope: Do not fraternize with the hot-tempered man, nor approach him to converse. (11,12)

25

The Davidic Ancestry of Jesus Christ

There are two accounts of the ancestry of Jesus Christ. One is found in Matthew; the other is in Luke. For those who take the Bible literally, the two lists are accurate, though different. The literalist might introduce an article of explanation in this way:

> *The genealogy of Jesus Christ has been a topic for discussion for many years. Matthew gives one account of the lineage of Christ while Luke gives another. The two accounts are different. Does this mean that there is a contradiction within the Bible? If there is a contradiction, does that indicate that the Bible is not the inspired word of God? If the Bible is not inspired by God, then the Bible is truly myth. The purpose of this article is to prove that the two accounts of Christ's genealogy are not a contradiction at all;, rather both accounts are totally accurate. This also leads to the Bible indeed being the inspired word of God, and therefore not myth.*

The hypothetical article of explanation would then try to show that the list of ancestors in Luke are traceable through Mary, whereas the ancestry list of Matthew works back from Joseph. Interesting view, but unacceptable to historical-critical research.

It might serve some purpose to list the ancestors that each gospel writer gives. However, we would be assuming that the lists are truly historical, being based on Old Testament information. Since we have seen many instances of Old Testament history turn out to be fabricated, the accuracy of such information would immediately be brought into question.

Let us examine the list in Matthew. The genealogy has three parts, with each section supposed to have 14 generations. Benedict Viviano, O.P., in the JBC 42: 9, suggests that the numerical pattern imposed could involve the numerical value of the consonants in the Hebrew of David's name dwd ($d = 4$, $w = 6$)...so $4 + 6 + 4 = 14$. Thus, the whole list would be Davidic.

Matthew's list contains the names of several women, an unusual way of listing one's ancestry. Further, while most of the names come from biblical sources, there are some that do not. There are names that may come from oral tradition which are not known to have been genealogically related.

As regards the list in Luke, unlike that in Matthew which occurs at the gospel's outset, it is found after the infancy narrative and the baptism of Jesus at the end of chapter 3. These lists are identical between Abraham and David, but they differ radically from that point onward.

The discrepancies between the two lists are obvious to the historical-critical scholar. Some have suggested that the lists are simply fabrications constructed from known genealogical relationships and improvised additions. There has been no definitive confirmation of the historical accuracy of either list.

Luke records in chapter 2 that Caesar's decree for a world-wide census required that Joseph was to be enrolled in the city of David called Bethlehem, "because he was of the house and family of David." According to 1 Samuel 17: 12, David was the son of an Ephrathite named Jesse, who was from Bethlehem in Judah; so, according to scripture, David's birthplace was Bethlehem.

The question anyone might raise would be: *How many descendants of David were there at the time of Christ's birth?* Certainly it is not unreasonable that after a millennium there would have been thousands (some have suggested 1,000,000!) who descended from David, and would have to have gone to Bethlehem to register. "No room in the inn," would have been an understatement!

Yet, the practical problem is this: Who can trace his / her lineage back more than four of five generations today, even with written birth or baptismal records? I have tried to find lineage for my surname's family, even going back to the town in Germany where my great-great grandfather was married early in the 1800s, only to find that the baptismal record of Jacob Hahnenberg had been destroyed in a fire during WWII. Failing that, I only have the oral tradition of stories, not about my great-great grandfather or my great grandfather, but only about my grandfather, told me by my father.

However, the gospels are, to the person of Christian faith, divinely inspired. So, whether the genealogies are accurately historical or constructs based on Old Testament references, with names added or omitted to fill a mathematical model reflecting a rabbinical technique called *gematria,* faith dictates that Jesus descended from David, (taking on his human nature from Mary), as prophesied in Isaiah 9: 5–6:

> *For a child is born to us, a son is given us; upon his shoulder dominion rests. They name him Wonder-Counselor, God-Hero, Father-Forever, Prince of Peace. His dominion is vast and forever peaceful, From David's throne, and over his kingdom, which he confirms and sustains By judgment and justice, both now and forever. The zeal of the LORD of hosts will do this!* (NAB: Isaiah 9: 5–6)

26

The Gospels

If one is looking for historical continuity in the gospels, there are interesting issues that come to the forefront. In a book by Burton H. Throckmorton, Jr. *Gospel Parallels: A Comparison of the Synoptic Gospels* (Thomas Nelson, Inc., 1992), the book's format gives parallel columns of Matthew, Mark, and Luke and cross-references events recorded in these gospels. For example, each of the versions of the healing of the paralytic is listed, so one can read the versions of each of the three gospels and compare how, and at what point in the gospel, the event was described by each of the three gospel writers.

Matthew, Mark, and Luke are referred to as the **synoptic gospels** (from Greek, συν, *syn*, together, and ὄπσις, *opsis*, seeing), or gospels written with the "same eye." Church historian Eusebius (c. 263–339 AD) devised a method that enabled scholars to find parallel texts. In the 5th century, Augustine of Hippo developed what was later known as the Augustinian hypothesis, which proposed why these three gospels were so similar.

In the synoptics, there are similarities in the description of events in Jesus' life, as well as differences. A perusal of Throckmorton's book gives an excellent insight into the way in which the three gospel writers described (or omitted) events.

In some cases, one writer will record an event in the life of Christ with considerable detail, yet that event will be omitted in another's gospel, or summarized concisely. In addition, the chronology of the synoptics, while generally in sync, has the same event occurring at different times in the life of Jesus. We have already seen how Matthew begins his gospel with the genealogy of Jesus, whereas Luke places the genealogy after the infancy narrative.

When one looks at the gospel of John, we see a different chronology than found in the synoptics, plus additional material not found in the Matthew, Mark, and Luke. John contains more theological discourses. The intimate Last Supper discourse in John finds no parallel in the synoptics. The differences between all of the gospels are seen in the accounts of the Resurrection. In the four gospels, there are five variant accounts of the Resurrection. (Mark 16: 1–8 differs from Mark 16: 9–20.) The JBC shows the different accounts in parallel columns in 81: 131. Though the differences are slight, one example of detail in Mark which differs from that in Luke is the visual picture of "the stone rolled back; youth sitting inside on right" found in Mark 16: 1–8 compared with "the stone rolled back: two men standing (inside); angels."

How does the historical-critical scholar view differences in gospel descriptions and chronology?

One of the best historical-critical scholars was Raymond E. Brown, S.S. (1928–1998). Brown was the editor of the JBC, and appointed member of the Pontifical Biblical Commission in 1972 and again in 1996. His work, *An Introduction to the New Testament*, Doubleday, 1997, is, by his own admission, an introductory work "not written for fellow scholars," but for "Bible study groups, religious education, college surveys, and initial seminary classes." Nevertheless, it is a scholarly work, and this author highly recommends it as the best introduction to the New Testament from an historical-critical viewpoint. Brown was one of the first Catholic scholars in the United States to use the historical-critical method to study the Bible.

Brown would assert first of all, that the gospels are dated to different decades following the earthly life of Jesus. Assuming, as Brown's JBC does, that Jesus died in 30 AD, the first gospel to have been written was that of Mark, in the 60s; that of Matthew and Luke in the 80s; and that of John in the 90s.

Thus, there would have been a period of more than thirty years before the first gospel was written and more than sixty years before the last. What happened in the time between the death of Jesus and the first gospel was the development of oral traditions that began with the apostles and those who had witnessed the events of Jesus firsthand. As might be expected, the oral stories were stories about Jesus related with the ordinary differences in accounts that occur when stories are repeated.

There was no TV coverage nor digital pictures of the events recorded in the gospels. There apparently were many written accounts, which were not gospels nor apocryphal works, which were available to the gospel writers. (Interestingly, Paul was the first to record anything in the New Testament in 1 Thessalonians in 51 AD.)

Testimony to the oral and written sources comes from Luke who begins his gospel with the following, verses 1–4:

> *Since many have undertaken to compile a narrative of the events that have been fulfilled among us, just as those who were eyewitnesses from the beginning and ministers of the word have handed them down to us, I too have decided, after investigating everything accurately anew, to write it down in an orderly sequence for you, most excellent Theophilus, so that you may realize the certainty of the teachings you have received.* (NAB: Luke 1: 1–4)

In addition to diverse accounts, both oral and written which were available to the gospel writers, including the hypothetical "Q" (*quelle* – source) material which is thought to have existed, when they attempted to recount the extraordinary life of Jesus Christ, they chose to focus on a thematic design. Each writer had a purpose in mind when they were written. Matthew is generally thought of as having been written to a Jewish audience that is at least familiar with Christianity, while Mark is more for Gentiles (non-Jews).

Luke develops the picture of Jesus' identity and mission in the marvelous and powerful scene of the keynote address in Nazareth (4:14–30). Scripture scholars help us to appreciate Luke's creativity as artist and as theologian. Writing his Gospel many years after the death and resurrection of Jesus, Luke wanted to share his community's experience and commitment and vision. So he felt free to rearrange his primary source, Mark's Gospel, by moving this Nazareth synagogue scene (Mark 6:1ff) to the very beginning of Jesus' public ministry (Luke 4:14ff). Luke's creativity is also found within the text itself, as he weaves together selections from several different chapters of Isaiah and omits some other points. As it stands, the exact text Luke puts on Jesus' lips would not be found on a synagogue scroll.

This passage (Luke 4: 14–30) is truly a keynote, establishing the basic themes of Luke's Gospel. Jesus, the anointed one (the Messiah, the Christ), teaches and heals and proclaims the presence of God's Reign. Jesus is the fulfillment of God's promises for the hungry, the sick, the imprisoned.

John is by far the most distinct and his writing is to an audience in need of more theological teaching. However, there is a uniqueness in John's main message…that Jesus is God. The synoptics do not mention this essential teaching. In John 1: 1–5, we see him begin this theme quite directly:

> *In the beginning was the Word, and the Word was*
> *with God, and the Word was God. He was in the*
> *beginning with God. All things came to be through*

> *him, and without him nothing came to be. What came*
> *to be through him was life, and this life was the light*
> *of the human race; the light shines in the darkness,*
> *and the darkness has not overcome it.* (NAB: John
> 1: 1–5)

In the execution of these writings, events in Jesus' life were arranged best to fit the focus of each of the evangelists, as we noted in Luke's version. In Matthew's gospel we see Jesus accomplishing his public ministry in days, not years! Everything has an urgency to it, and all leads up to the final days in Jerusalem. Matthew's chapters 5–7 contain Jesus teaching on a variety of subjects, with no reference as to when they occurred. Galilee is the setting for most of Jesus' ministry, culminating for his ministry in Jerusalem, the goal of his work. This final stage of his ministry lasts only a few days. It is then that Jesus cleanses the Temple of moneychangers, is arrested, and suffers crucifixion. It is of interest that John's gospel has the Temple cleansing at the beginning of Jesus' public ministry (John 2: 13–25).

Mark, considered to have been the main source material for Matthew and Luke, also conveys a sense of compact ministerial time. It is the shortest of all four of the gospels. In Mark, Jesus begins his ministry by calling the two sets of brothers (Andrew-Simon and James-John) by the Sea of Galilee. The journey then takes them to Capernaum and the Sabbath. Jesus teaches and drives an unclean spirit out in the synagogue. On leaving the synagogue, he enters the house of Simon and Andrew with the other two brothers and cures Simon's mother-in-law. That evening, the whole town gathers at the door and cures many who were sick and drives out many demons.

If one compares the call of the apostles in the other three gospels, the chronology differs. If one attempts to give an accurate chronology of the events surrounding the apostles' call, it is impossible to do so, because the differences are so obvious.

A simple question, "How long was Jesus' public ministry," has been traditionally answered as "three years." However, even that answer is questioned by historical-critical scholars. The common understanding is that Jesus' public ministry lasted a little over three years, largely due to the references in John. However, Luke identifies the fifteenth year of the reign of Tiberius Caesar as the anchor year for John the Baptist's appearance. Tiberius succeeded Augustus as emperor in 14 AD and reigned until 37 AD. The fifteenth year would have fallen somewhere between 28 and 29 AD. If Jesus' public ministry begins with his baptism by the Baptist, 29 AD would seem to be a reasonable choice. Further, it is known that Jesus was crucified sometime between 26 and 36 AD, because this was the period of Pontius Pilate's governorship. Complex astronomical calculations reveal that during this period Nisan 14 (Friday after Passover) fell on Friday twice, in 30 and 33 AD. So, why not 33 AD, instead of 30 AD for the year of Jesus' death? This date would fit the three year public ministry theory. Two reasons: First, the relatives of Jesus did not believe in him (John 7: 5), even after the second Passover (John 6: 4). If Nazareth, only twenty miles from the Sea of Galilee, was the town near which his relatives lived, they certainly would have been curious to see him work a miracle. They would have heard about his miraculous powers in the space of a year. However, if the miracles, which occurred mostly in the triangle of towns bordering the Sea of Galilee (Capernaum, Bethsaida, and Chorazin...all within a few hours walk from each other), had been performed in a few months' time, their skepticism might be understandable. Second, chapter six of John begins with the feeding of the 5000, followed by the discourse on the bread of life. It is this author's opinion that placing the event of the Passover (the feast of unleavened bread) at the beginning of chapter 6 was an etiological method of tying the Old Testament to the church's tradition of Eucharistic celebration. Therefore, whether there really were three Passovers is open to question. Several scholars place the date of Jesus' death at 30 AD. Thus, John's second Passover would have been a literary device rather than a real event. It is interesting, finally, to note that there are two extreme views found in the early church fathers as to the length of the ministry of Jesus: St. Irenaeus (Contra Haer., II, xxii, 3–6) appears to suggest a period of fifteen years; the prophetic phrases, "the year of recompenses", "the year of my redemption" (Is., xxxiv, 8; lxiii, 4), appear to have persuaded Clement of Alexandria, Julius Africanus, Philastrius, Hilarion, and two or three other patristic writers to allow only one year for the public life.

The current thinking of some scholars is that the public ministry of Jesus may have been anywhere from one to four years. John 2:20 suggests a relationship of Jesus' ministry with the 46th year of the Temple reconstruction (26 AD). The JBC deals with the uncertain issue in 75: 169–170.

Scholars have come with a myriad of theories as to the relationship of the synoptic gospels with each other. A fascinating website addressing the "Synoptic Problem," assembled by Stephen C. Carlson, is to found at: http://www.mindspring.com/~scarlson/synopt/index.html. As we have noted, St. Augustine saw the similarities in the three gospels. He hypothesized that Matthew's gospel was the first written, then Mark used Matthew, and, finally, Luke used both Matthew and Mark. Although Augustine's hypothesis is rejected today by historical-critical scholars, Augustine might be considered the father of the Synoptic Problem...a problem that has as yet found no satisfactory solution.

27

The "Hidden" Gospels

There has been a recent fascination with the gospels that did not make the Christian canon of inspired books in the New Testament. These are referred to as the apocryphal or "hidden" gospels. (Protestants use *pseudopigraphal* to designate *apocryphal*; whereas, Protestant *apocryphal* works are Catholic *deuterocanonical*.)

The "hidden" gospels can be divided into three categories: those relating to the history of Mary and Joseph, the infancy of Christ, and the history of Pilate. Most of these are based on the *Protevangelium of James*, *the Gospel of Thomas*, and the *Acts of Pilate*. The main apocryphal (pseudopigraphal) gospels are:

- **Gospel of Thomas**—Some may refer to the Gospel of Thomas as the fifth gospel. This is a Gnostic writing, though some scholars may see some of the sayings of Jesus in this gospel as genuine. There are 114 sayings attributed to Jesus in the Gospel of Thomas.
- **The Infancy Gospel of Thomas**
- **The Protoevangelium of James**
- **The Gospel of Mary Magdalene**
- **The Gospel of Peter**
- **The Gospel of Philip**
- **The Gospel of Nicodemus**
- **The Gospel of Hebrews**
- **The Gospel of the Egyptians**
- **The Gospel of the Ebionites**

- **The Gospel of the Nazoreans**

Why did the early church reject these writings? Larely, because they were written by followers of Gnosticism. Gnosticism (from Greek *gnōsis*, knowledge) refers to a religious movement consisting of various belief systems generally united in the teaching that humans are divine souls trapped in a material world. In order to free oneself from the inferior material world, one needs knowledge given only to the few.

For example, a Gnostic gospel of the second century is The Gospel of Mary Magdalene promoted in *The Da Vinci Code* by Dan Brown. A key point of Brown's proposed theory is found in the Gospel of Mary Magdalene has to do with Jesus' favoritism toward her. The text seems to reflect a conflict where Peter was challenging the role of Mary as a recipient of a special revelation from Jesus. Mary was distraught about Peter's challenge. The implication here is that Jesus knew Mary well enough to consider her worthy to be the recipient of special revelation.

The main passage that Brown uses as support actually comes from one of these Gnostic writings (Gospel of Philip 63:32–64:10). This text describes Mary Magdalene as a "companion" of Jesus. History tells us that this text from the Gospel of Philip, as well as other Gnostic texts, was composed in the second half of the third century. This is a full two hundred years after the life of Jesus. The passage that Brown uses as his premise has many missing elements.

Note that although the Gospel of Mary is not considered to be inspired, Brown interprets the text with his own twists. In fact, there was no mention of Jesus being married to Mary or of them having an intimate relationship. This text simply says that Jesus appeared to her alone. This is not against the biblical story of Jesus revealing Himself to Mary after His resurrection. Where Brown escapes fact is when he begins filling in words randomly, all the while having the reader believe them to be true, verifiable fact.

The Gospel of Mary, because only one copy was recovered, will likely never be a complete and historically verifiable document. The canonized Scriptures are based on multiple copies passed down through the generations and discovered in various locations. If we offer up the Gospel of Mary to be anything other than literary fiction, historians would require there to be factual evidence to support such a claim, not only the opinion of Dan Brown, a fiction novel writer.

Another apocryphal gospel is the Gospel of Thomas. Many Sayings in Thomas have parallels with the New Testament sayings, especially those found in the synoptic gospels. This leads many to believe that Thomas was also based on "Q." Indeed, some have speculated that Thomas may in fact be "Q". Unlike the synoptic Gospels, and like "Q", the Gospel of Thomas has no narrative connecting the various Sayings. In form, it is simply a list of 114 Sayings, in no particular order. 79 of these Sayings have some parallel with the synoptics. Comparison with New Testament parallels show that Thomas contains either more primitive versions of the Sayings, or developments of more primitive versions. Either way, Thomas seems to preserve earlier traditions about Jesus than the New Testament. Although it is not possible to attribute the Gospel of Thomas to any particular sect, it is clearly Gnostic in nature. As the preamble indicates, these are "secret sayings," and are intended to be esoteric in nature.

Not to be confused with the Gospel of Thomas is the Infancy Gospel of Thomas. It is, like many such texts, an apocryphal work. It claims within itself to have been written by Thomas the Israelite, and it is judged not to have been written by the same author as that of the Gospel of Thomas. The apostle Thomas is very unlikely to have had anything to do with the text. Whoever its initial author was, he seems not to have known much of Jewish life besides what he could learn from the Gospel of Luke. The beginning of the apocryphal work gives this description of the child Jesus when he was five years old: (*The Infancy Gospel of Thomas* as translated by Harold Attridge & Ronald F. Hock in the book *The Complete Gospels*, Harper Collins, 1992.)

When this boy, Jesus, was five years old, he was playing at the ford of a rushing stream. He was collecting the flowing water into ponds and made the water instantly pure. He did this with a single command. He then made soft clay and shaped it into twelve sparrows. He did this on the Sabbath day, and many other boys were playing with him.

But when a Jew saw what Jesus was doing while playing on the sabbath day, he immediately went off and told Joseph, Jesus' father: "See here, your boy is at the ford and has taken mud and fashioned twelve birds with it, and so has violated the sabbath."

So Joseph went there, and as soon as he spotted him he shouted, "Why are you doing what's not permitted on the sabbath?"

But Jesus simply clapped his hands and shouted to the sparrows: "Be off, fly away, and remember me, you who are now alive!" And the sparrows took off and flew away noisily.

The Jews watched with amazement, then left the scene to report to their leaders what they had seen Jesus doing.

The son of Annas the scholar, standing there with Jesus, took a willow branch and drained the water Jesus had collected. Jesus, however, saw what had happened and became angry, saying to him, "Damn you, you irreverent fool! What harm did the ponds of water do to you? From this moment you, too, will dry up like a tree, and you'll never produce leaves or root or bear fruit."

In an instant the boy had completely withered away. Then Jesus departed and left for the house of Joseph. The parents of the boy who had withered away picked him up and were carrying him out, sad because he was so young. And they came to Joseph and accused him: "It's your fault—your boy did this."

Later he was going through the village again when a boy ran and bumped him on the shoulder. Jesus got angry and said to him, "You won't continue your journey." And all of a sudden, he fell down and died.

Some people saw what had happened and said, "Where has this boy come from? Everything he says happens instantly!" The parents of the dead boy came to Joseph and blamed him saying, "Because you have such a boy, you can't live with us in the village, or else teach him to bless and not curse. He's killing our children!"

So Joseph summoned his child and admonished him in private, saying, "Why are you doing all this? These people are suffering and so they hate and harass us." Jesus said, "I know that these are not your words, still, I'll keep quiet for your sake. But those people must take their punishment." There and then his accusers became blind. Those who saw this became very fearful and at a loss. All they could say was, "Every word he says, whether good or bad, has became a deed—a miracle even!"

When Joseph saw that Jesus had done such a thing, he got angry and grabbed his ear and pulled very hard. The boy became infuriated with him and replied, "It's one thing for you to seek and not find; it's quite another for you to act this unwisely. Don't you know that I don't really belong to you? Don't make me upset."

When one reads the above, one is struck by the impression that Jesus is a spoiled brat with miraculous powers. It is easy to see why it was rejected by the early church.

Some of the material in the apocryphal gospels has found its way into the early Catholic Christian tradition. In the *Protevangelium of James*, the author explains the issue of whether Mary had other children than Jesus. According to the *Protevangelium*, Joseph had children by a previous marriage, whence the "brothers of Jesus" in Matthew 12: 46–49. St. Jerome, however, played on the word in Greek for "brothers," *adelphoi*, which, he maintained had the meaning of "cousin."

That Mary was a virgin at Jesus' birth is attested by the *Protevngelium*. The virginity of Mary, before, during, and after the birth of Jesus is a dogma of the Catholic and Orthodox Churches. Also mentioned in the *Protevangelium* are the names of the parents of Mary, Joachim and Anna, whose feasts are celebrated in the Catholic Church on July 26th and in the Orthodox Church on September 9th each year.

28

New Testament Authorship

For almost two millennia, two of the four evangelists, Matthew and John, were thought to have been eyewitnesses to the events in Jesus' life because they were apostles. In addition, the Pauline epistles were thought to include the Epistle to the Hebrews. The apostle John was also thought to have written the three Johannine epistles, as well as the Book of Revelation.

However, as these texts were analyzed in the twentieth century, questions arose as to the style of writing used by these writers, leading to questions about the true authors of several of the works in the New Testament.

As indicated above, historical-critical scholars have, for the most part, concluded that Mark's gospel was the first to have been written. Matthew's gospel seems to have copied from Mark with some modifications. It is now commonly thought that in its present form, the Gospel of Matthew is not the work of an eyewitness apostle. Why would an eyewitness need to copy from someone like Mark who was not an eyewitness? However, Papias of Hierapolis, writing early in the second century stated that Matthew compiled the Sayings of Jesus in the Aramaic language and "everyone translated them as well as he could."

As regards the gospel of John, some historical-critical scholars have concluded that, while it probably is the work of one author (with some editing by others), its Christology is well beyond what would have been likely for a fisherman. Irenaeus of Lyons (d. 202 AD) defended the authorship of the gospel by the apostle John. However Eusebius (referred to above) noted that Irenaeus had confused two different persons named John. Some scholars have suggested that the Gospel of John reflects the apostle's theology which was later written down under the influence of a community which had ties to the apostle. Raymond E. Brown S.S., regarded as a specialist concerning the hypothetical 'Johannine community,' speculated that this community contributed to the authorship of the Gospel of John. He taught the development of a Johannine church from which came the Gospel of John, composed after the crisis caused by the expulsion of Christians from the synagogue. Possibly the original community moved to Ephesus, which later church tradition assigned to Johannine Christianity.

As to the authorship of the three Johannine epistles, many exegetes speculate that 1 John was written to help understand the gospel tradition. This author may have done editing of the gospel itself. Comparison of the epistles with the gospel have led to the conclusion that the author is not the same.

Linguistic analyses of the Book of Revelation have led to the conclusions that there are great differences between it and the gospel, both as to style and use of the Greek. Several scholars have concluded that the author of Revelation was not that of the Johannine gospel or epistles, but an early unknown Christian prophet by the name of John…this conclusion, despite the early church fathers' opinion that the author of Revelation was the apostle John.

As to the author of the Epistle to the Hebrews, it was thought to be Paul as early as the end of the 2nd century. The early opinion was that Paul wrote it in Hebrew and then the epistle was translated into Greek by Luke. Origen pointed out differences between the other Pauline letters and the epistle to the Hebrews. Tertullian thought it to have been written by Barnabas. Erasmus, in the 16th century, raised doubts about its authorship. Today, it is commonly held by scholars that Paul is neither directly or indirectly the author.

The issue of authorship of the above canonical books of the New Testament has little to do with their divine inspiration. The 27 books of the New Testament are all considered divinely inspired by mainline Christians. The question that might arise would be if a "lost" epistle of Paul were ever found, which is considered possible. Would that work be considered part of the canon? At this time, for the most part, Christianity considers the canon to be closed.

29

Numeric Symbolism in the New Testament

Whether one thinks about seven days in a week or a "lucky seven" roll of the dice, it seems the number seven is a special number even today. The number 7 is used over four hundred times in the Bible. However, the number 3 is used nearly five hundred times, the number 2 eight hundred, and the number 1 over three thousand.

Seven, however, is quite special. In the New Testament, it can have a literal meaning, but more often, a symbolic one. A quote from the New Testament will illustrate:

> Then Peter approaching asked him, "Lord, if my brother sins against me, how often must I forgive him? As many as seven times?" Jesus answered, "I say to you, not seven times but seventy-seven times."
> (NAB: Matthew 18:21–22)

Peter's meaning of seven in this context is "repeatedly." Jesus uses a multiple of the number as if to teach that forgiveness knows no set limit.

We find the number seven used in another setting (Matthew 15: 36–37) when Jesus feeds the people with seven loaves of bread and a few fish, with seven baskets left over.

The question posed by the Sadducees about which of seven deceased brothers would have as his wife the woman they each married in the resurrection of the body (which the Sadducees rejected)...why the use of seven?

The Book of Revelation has many "sevens." The book is addressed to seven churches by the author with "grace to you and peace from him who is and who was and who is to come, and from the seven spirits before his throne..." Seven gold lamp stands, seven stars, seven flaming torches, seven seals, seven horns, seven eyes, seven trumpets, seven thunders, seven thousand people killed in an earthquake, a dragon with seven heads with seven diadems, seven last plagues, seven gold bowls, seven hills, seven kings...all are images in the apocalyptic book. Again, why the number seven?

In the Old Testament, God creates the world in six days and rests on the seventh. A sense of "wholeness" or "completeness"... even "perfection" seems to be symbolized. Yet in the Book of Revelation, seven is associated with death, plagues, and a dragon; a sense of doom is created by the images, rather than one of wholeness or completeness.

Even though seven is used in a negative sense, it still would not be used in those instances to indicate anything other than something "complete," though "imperfect."

Three and twelve also have the meaning of "complete." The number 30, in reference to Jesus beginning his public life was a number to indicate "mature adulthood." The number 40 was used to indicate a "generation." The number 1000 was considered an infinite amount. So, for example, in the Book of Revelation, the number 144,000 means "12" X "12" (a complete, perfect number...patterned after the Twelve tribes of Israel and Twelve apostles) X "1000" = a virtually uncountable number. The numbers used in the New Testament are filled with symbolism and generally are not to be taken literally.

30

The Inerrancy
of Scripture

In the doctrinal statement of a well-known Midwest Evangelical university, one of the tenents reads: *WE BELIEVE that God has revealed Himself and His truth in the created order, in the Scriptures, and supremely in Jesus Christ; and that the Scriptures of the Old and New Testaments are verbally inspired by God and inerrant in the original writing, so that they are fully trustworthy and of supreme and final authority in all they say.*

The issue fundamentalists cling to is the "inerrancy" of Scripture. N.L.Geisler, in "Inerrancy and Free Will," *EVQ* 57 (1985) 350–351 states:

> *Inerrancy follows from divine authority, period. For whatever god utters is without error. And the Bible is the Word of God. Therefore, the Bible is without error. But if this is so, then the inerrancy of the Bible cannot be lost by simply adding the human dimension. As long as it is God's Word, then it is thereby inerrant, whether or not it is also the words of men.*

What is inerrancy of the Bible? Inerrancy of the Bible is the quality attributed to Scripture that the original words written by the authors of the Bible are free from error because of divine inspiration. The more fundamentalist one is, the more is rejected any possible error historically or theologically in the words of Scripture. There are "enlightened" fundamentalists who recognize, through historical criticism, discrepancies in biblical manuscripts, but that through various harmonizations and metaphorical readings, verbal inerrancy can be maintained.

Protestants generally accept Luther's *sola scriptura*, i.e. Scripture is the only source of truth for Christians' salvation. Yet, most mainline Protestant scholars are comfortable with the historical-critical method. Their concept of "inerrancy" parallels that found in Catholic historical-critical scholarship.

So, what is the Catholic position on "inerrancy"? While the Catholic Church's position has shifted from a more fundamentalist and literalist interpretation of Scripture found in past centuries, Vatican II's *Dei Verbum*, Chapter III, sections 11 and 12 state:

> *11. Those divinely revealed realities which are contained and presented in Sacred Scripture have been committed to writing under the inspiration of the Holy Spirit. For holy mother Church, relying on the belief of the Apostles (see John 20:31; 2 Tim. 3:16; 2 Peter 1:19–20, 3:15–16), holds that the books of both the Old and New Testaments in their entirety, with all their parts, are sacred and canonical because written under the inspiration of the Holy Spirit, they have God as their author and have been handed on as such to the Church herself. In composing the sacred books, God chose men and while employed by Him they made use of their powers and abilities, so that with Him acting in them and through them, they, as true authors, consigned to writing everything and only those things which He wanted.*

> *Therefore, since everything asserted by the inspired*

authors or sacred writers must be held to be asserted by the Holy Spirit, it follows that the books of Scripture must be acknowledged as teaching solidly, faithfully and without error that truth which God wanted put into sacred writings for the sake of salvation. Therefore "all Scripture is divinely inspired and has its use for teaching the truth and refuting error, for reformation of manners and discipline in right living, so that the man who belongs to God may be efficient and equipped for good work of every kind" (2 Tim. 3:16–17, Greek text).

12. However, since God speaks in Sacred Scripture through men in human fashion, the interpreter of Sacred Scripture, in order to see clearly what God wanted to communicate to us, should carefully investigate what meaning the sacred writers really intended, and what God wanted to manifest by means of their words.

To search out the intention of the sacred writers, attention should be given, among other things, to "literary forms." For truth is set forth and expressed differently in texts which are variously historical, prophetic, poetic, or of other forms of discourse. The interpreter must investigate what meaning the sacred writer intended to express and actually expressed in particular circumstances by using contemporary literary forms in accordance with the situation of his own time and culture. For the correct understanding of what the sacred author wanted to assert, due attention must be paid to the customary and characteristic styles of feeling, speaking and narrating which prevailed at the time of the sacred writer, and to the patterns men normally employed at that period in their everyday dealings with one another.

In addition, Catholics look to two sources of truth…Scripture and tradition. What is meant by "tradition" in this context is defined in the *Catechism of the Catholic Church,* Liguori Publications, 1994:

> *In order that the full and living Gospel might always be preserved in the Church the apostles left bishops as their successors. They gave them their own position of teaching authority. Indeed, "the apostolic preaching, which is expressed in a special way in the inspired books, was to be preserved in a continuous line of succession until the end of time.*

> *This living transmission, accomplished in the Holy Spirit, is called Tradition, since it is distinct from Sacred Scripture, though closely connected to it. Through Tradition, "the Church, in her doctrine, life and worship, perpetuates and transmits to every generation all that she herself is, all that she believes." The sayings of the holy Fathers are a witness to the life-giving presence of this Tradition, showing how its riches are poured out in the practice and life of the Church, in her belief and her prayer.* (CCC: 77–78)

An example of Tradition would be the doctrine of the Mary's Immaculate Conception or her Assumption into Heaven. Though not mentioned in the Bible, these teachings have infallible status as dogmas of the Catholic Church.

In summary, fundamentalist Protestants are more inclined to accept the inerrancy of the Bible in all its aspects, whereas mainline Protestant, Orthodox, and Catholic scholars look to the truths contained in Scripture necessary for salvation as inerrant.

31

How Far is Too Far?

As a Catholic teacher of young and elderly adults for the past forty-five years, I am keenly aware of how disturbing, particularly to older adults, the historical-critical method's conclusions can be. I particularly remember a bible study I taught wherein I explained the Book of Jonah as didactic fiction. Having finished, I thought the twenty-some adults would gratefully agree that the historical-critical explanation of the meaning of the book was an improvement over the literal. In seeking feedback, I was satisfied that I had succeeded in enlightening them, when one lady remarked, "I think I'll stick with the literal interpretation, just to be safe!"

As a secondary school administrator in both public and parochial school systems, I have always been interested in students' growth in education. Mandated curricula in the U.S. K–12 was the topic of my Ed. S. dissertation, and while a social studies teacher, I was concerned with the growth of my students' knowledge in courses I taught, such as American History and Comparative World Religions.

Even today, in retirement from secondary school teaching and administration, I continue to teach adults. I am convinced that the pursuit of truth should never end, no matter one's age.

I have an hypothesis that our public and parochial schools do a far better job at advancing knowledge to its youth in mathematics, the social sciences, and language than Christianity does in teaching its dogmas and truths to the young. Aside from some mandatory preparatory classes for Baptism and Marriage, adult education in the faith is a voluntary thing. What little is learned about one's religion is restricted to the 15 minute homily or sermon on Sundays. For example, the average Catholic receives, at the most, ten to fifteen hours of formal homiletic exposure during the course of a year. The homily is not intended for instruction primarily, but for inspiration, using the biblical texts as the starting point.

I am well aware how difficult it is to have an attentive audience for more than fifteen minutes, much less a fifty-five minute class period. Homilists face similar challenges, but often with much larger groups. Yet, like some teachers, they often lower the bar of effective communication below mediocrity, either reading their text or "winging it," with generic verbiage that is less than inspiring.

In Canon 747 of the Code of Canon Law, the content of the homily is concisely stated: "...in the homily the mysteries of faith and the norms of Christian living are to be expounded from the sacred text." Consequently, the oft-taken course by the homilist is to retell the sacred texts. This technique comes across as to make one wonder whether Jesus or the sacred authors "got it right" in the first place. Sadly, homilies are often platitudinous "sacred Muzak," with the faithful dutifully listening to the homilist, but glancing at their watches if the homily goes beyond ten minutes.

So, if my hypothesis is correct, something must be done for the good of the faithful, particularly in instruction in how to understand the Bible.

In 1961 and 1964 the Pontifical Biblical Commission's Instructions both insisted on the dangers of scandalizing the faithful in bible study with "vain and insufficiently established novelties." These warnings have a point. If someone from the pulpit were to state: "There was no Garden of Eden," that kind of unsubstantiated statement would not only shock, but would divide the faithful.

The New Jerome Biblical Commentary (JBC), to which I have often referred, has some sound advice. I will end this book with the following lengthy, but extremely important quote from the JBC:

> *An excessively negative popular presentation of the results of biblical criticism is not only dangerous for the faithful but does damage to reputable biblical scholars by popularizing their views without necessary qualifications and in a context where those views were never meant to be presented. The general principle is that one should not leave the audience with problems that the audience is not capable of solving. If one brings in elements of historical criticism, then one should take cognizance of possible implications and head off wrong conclusions.*
>
> *But if we acknowledge the danger of rash popularization, we must firmly accentuate the danger on the other side as well—a danger that unfortunately has not received sufficient attention in church documents. This is the danger that an exaggerated fear of scandal will prevent popularizers from communicating to educated Catholics the more sophisticated understanding of the Bible that they should have. So often we hear about the few that are scandalized, and no voice is raised about the much greater crime of leaving the many in ignorance of modern biblical criticism. Fear of scandal must never lead to a double standards whereby the simple or the young are taught things about the Bible that are false*

just that they will not be shocked. Common sense dictates that all education be scaled to the ability of the audience, but this does not mean that elementary biblical instruction should be noncritical. It means that elementary instruction should be critical in an elementary way. From the very first time the story of Gen 1–3 is told to kindergarten children, they should be taught to think of it as a popular story and not as history, even though the teacher may not wish at that level to raise formally the question of historicity. Even beginners can be taught to think of the Gospels as recorded preaching and teaching rather than as biographies of Jesus.

Unfortunately too, an exaggerated fear of scandal can hamper scientific research. There are a host of delicate biblical questions that need scientific study and discussion...Yet scholars know that when they write on these subjects even in professional and technical journals, an account, often confused and sometimes hostile, will soon appear in the popular press. In other words, while competent Catholic scholars are urged by the church to keep these matters away from public notice, whether they like it or not, others will popularize their work. The result is that frequently the scholar is accused of being responsible for the scandal and is made the target of recriminations by would-be protectors of the faith. The whole distinction between discussion on a scholarly level and popularization—a distinction sometimes facilely proposed in warnings from Rome—is rapidly dying out; and we should face this problem more frankly and more practically. In the long run more damage has been done to the church by the fact that her scholars have not always been free to discuss delicate problems than by the fact that some of the faithful are scandalized by the lack of ideas than by the presence of new ideas. Imprudence and occasional scandal are the almost inevitable price that one must pay for the right of free discussion. And indeed such free academic discussion has its own way of crushing errors—a devastating book review in a biblical journal by a competent scholar may be more effective in eradicating nonsense than a warning from church authority that may seem simply to be repressive of freedom. (JBC 71: 90–92)

Bibliography

Brown, Raymond E. *An Introduction to the New Testament,* Doubleday, 1997.

Brown, Raymond E. et al. *The New Jerome Biblical Commentary,* Prentice Hall, 1990.

Catechism of the Catholic Church, Liguori Publications, 1994.

Coogan, Michael. *The Oxford History of the Biblical World,* Oxford University Press, 1998.

Dahood, Mitchell. *Psalms I: 1–50,* Doubleday, 1966.
      Psalms II: 51–100, Doubleday, 1968.
      Psalms III: 101–150, Doubleday, 1970.

Eerdman's Handbook to the World's Religions, Eerdmans Publishing, 1994.

Hahnenberg, Edward J. *The Evolution of Belief in the Afterlife in the Old Testament,* Wingspan Press, 2005.

Mazar, Amihai. *Archaeology of the Land of the Bible: 10,000–586 B.C.E.,* Doubleday, 1992.

Pritchard, James B., ed. *Ancient Near Eastern Texts,* Princeton University Press, 1969.

The Interpretation of the Bible in the Church. United States Catholic Conference, 1996.

The New American Bible. Catholic Bible Publishers, 1988.

Throckmorton Jr., Burton H. *Gospel Parallels: A Comparison of the Synoptic Gospels,* Thomas Nelson Publishers, 1992.

Vatican Council II: The Basic Sixteen Documents. Costello Publications, 1996.

Whybray, R. Norman. *Introduction to the Pentateuch,* Eerdmans Publishing, 1995.

CPSIA information can be obtained at www.ICGtesting.com
Printed in the USA
LVOW07s0144100216

474404LV00001B/1/P